Intermediate Guide to Whittling

15 Secrets Woodcarvers Should Know to Get Better

Ryan Feldman

professional advice. The content within this book has been derived from various sources. Please consult a licensed professional before attempting any techniques outlined in this book.

By reading this document, the reader agrees that under no circumstances is the author responsible for any losses, direct or indirect, that are incurred as a result of the use of the information contained within this document, including, but not limited to, errors, omissions, or inaccuracies.

Table of Contents

Introduction

I grabbed the mallet from its spot on the wall and marched back outside. After securing the wood to the table, I carefully held the chisel in one hand and swung the mallet. It connected to the back of the chisel with a dull thud and I marveled at how easily the chip came away from the piece. Swing for swing, I carved out a new design with a newfound confidence in my skills. I was proud of myself: No longer did I just whittle; a whole new world of possibilities opened in front of my eyes.

***

Whittling has always been my first love and saving grace. As far back as I can remember, I walked through the forests of the Pacific Northwest searching for sticks to create a masterpiece with nothing more than a simple pocket knife. I loved finding a new piece of wood and imagining the possibilities. For a while, I lost my way getting caught up in drugs and petty crimes until I found my way back to my home and wood. Truly, woodcarving saved my life and got me back onto the straight and narrow.

Wood remains ever-present in my life today, both as a career and a hobby. I consider myself to be a lumberjack and forged a career in carpentry where I build homes. On the side, I practice my hobby, woodcarving, and have started earning a sizable income from doing what I love. Now, I want to share my passion and knowledge with you!

So you already know the basics of whittling and now your fingers are itching to try more techniques. Yet, you may wonder what the difference is between whittling and woodcarving. Whittling is a specific technique within wood carving, which mainly uses basic knives and handheld pieces of wood. It is a basic technique, so I am going to empower you with everything you need to know to take your hobby to the next level.

"Carving is a source of joy to the artist...To attack the raw material, gradually to extract a shape out of it following one's own desire, or, sometimes, the inspiration of the material itself: this gives the sculptor great joy." - Aristide Maillol.

The quote above shows the joy that wood carving can bring to a person while giving insight into the process. The wood is a blank canvas that can become the masterpiece of your imagination. Are you ready to bring out your artistic side and express yourself through learning new techniques? Yes? Great! I am with you every step of the way.

In this book, I am going to take your skills one step further by introducing new wood carving techniques. Many whittlers get bored with the basic designs and start experimenting with other cuts and tools. Intricate designs and larger pieces become an aspirational goal, however, a lack of knowledge prevents you from creating matching artwork. The techniques I show throughout the book will expand your repertoire while using many of the tools you already have in your workshop. These techniques are an extension of whittling and do not require specialized tools, although I will present some options for expanding your collection.

There are 15 secrets to wood carving that I share with you throughout this book. These secrets are important elements of wood carving and many provide motivation to improve your skills. These secrets address all types of things including new techniques, the best tools for a specific job, and how to use wood and make proper cuts. Additional secrets consider sharpening stones, wood finishes, and practical wood carving tips. So, without further ado, here is the first secret you should know:

Secret 1: *Woodcarving isn't a craft that relies only on skill and technique. It's incredibly important for a carver to have patience. Rushing and getting frustrated because things are not going the way they should will truly get you nowhere. You need to make mistakes, you have to damage and break many pieces of wood until you become fully proficient.*

A few hours of wood carving each week can change your life and has so many benefits. Wood carving is a calming activity, which reduces stress, improves your breathing, and lowers your blood pressure. The more you focus on the rhythmic cuts, the more your mind settles and your body soon releases dopamine, a feel-good hormone. Working with wood creates a connection between you and nature, which is food for the soul. It is an activity away from technological influence where you can set your mind free and let creativity blossom. The feeling of pride upon finishing a piece is incomparable to anything else; it is a rush of energy!

Even if you do get frustrated when the wood breaks, it is part of the learning process and teaches patience. Take a quick break when you get stuck and get your mind back in the game. Sometimes, a few minutes away from your project gives clarity of mind and you realize where you are making mistakes. This is a great time to sharpen your tools or tidy your workspace. A break also gives your hands a rest from hard work because wood carving is harsh on your hands and sometimes you just need to release that tension.

Secret Two*: Whittling and general wood carving can tire your hands and wrists. Instead of suffering, seek methods that strengthen your grip and wrists. Squeeze a pressure ball while watching television, do hand exercises for improved range of motion, or strengthen your wrists with yoga exercises.*

Stronger hands make wood carving much easier but your hands also strengthen as you practice more. It helps in controlling the knife and other tools, which makes precision cutting easier resulting in a product with a high-quality finish. There are other ways to improve the end product, such as choosing the correct type of wood and a suitable finish.

I have added numerous projects for you to try in this book, which help in improving your new skills. So let's get started with the first new techniques and some practice designs. I cannot wait to teach you more about wood carving!

Chapter 1: Incised and Chip Carving Techniques

Whittling is the most basic wood carving technique that many of us learn from simply picking up a stick and hacking away at it with a knife. There is something magical about seeing the wood shavings flying all over the place. Once you have whittling under your belt, you can move onto new techniques and expand your skillset.

Some techniques necessitate a practiced hand for precise carving while using a range of tools. These techniques are suitable for individuals who have mastered intermediate techniques. Yet, you have to sharpen your skills (and knives) and grow your tool collection before learning advanced techniques. The next two chapters present these intermediate techniques for skill-building and act as a middle man between whittling and professional, complex wood carving.

Secret 3*: Incised carving, chip carving, intaglio, and relief carving are separate wood carving techniques. Yet, the tools used in all* *four techniques are quite similar. Additionally, their basics have a heavy dependence on whittling cuts and techniques. When whittling is the first wood carving technique a person masters, they often attempt other carving projects without any trouble at all.*

Incised Carving

Incised carving, sometimes called line carving, focuses on carving an outline. This technique reveals a two-dimensional image. A design or pattern is drawn onto a flat wood surface and then the outline is carved using specific tools. When I think about incised carving, it conjures images of school desks filled with graffiti. There was always something carved into the desk using a compass; a permanent memory for generations to come. Another familiar incised artwork is made by couples: a heart containing initials carved into the side of a tree. So, incised carving might be a technique that you have some knowledge of already. In its most simple form, it is a line.

Think back to your whittling techniques for a moment. A popular technique is the v-cut, which removes thin slivers of wood from your piece. Incised carving is similar to this method as it focuses on creating grooves, trenches, and lines. However, incised lines are thinner than v-cuts and are usually used on flat surfaces. You might have used a similar technique when adding details to your three-dimensional pieces, such as defining facial features.

Essential Tools

Although a simple pocket knife can work, specialized tools assist you in creating intricate incised designs. Gouges with a "v" or "u" shape and a veiner make incised carving a lot faster. The v-gouge produces an angled cut similar in shape to the results from a whittling v-cut. In contrast, the veiner and u-gouge generate a trench. Each design has its requirements regarding the best tool for the job, so read the instructions carefully or think about the design you want before starting. A veiner tends to produce a thinner line than gouges, so you might need a combination of tools for your design.

Practical Tips

Two tool grips are useful for incised carving: low grip and high grip. A low grip requires you to hold the tool at a small angle to the wood. The best way to do this is to hold the handle in the same way as you would a bicycle's handle. This grip is ideal for making long strokes using a push cut. With the high grip, hold the handle as if it was a pen so that there is a larger angle between the tool and wood. A high grip is necessary when working in tight areas and for creating curves or circles.

Decide on the depth of your carving before you start so that you know what you are working towards. Sometimes, shallow incisions will suffice but other designs require deeper cuts. A combination of depths is a sensible option too but determine the depth of each line so that there is consistency. There is nothing as bad as working hard and then realizing your piece is ruined by different line depths. Measure the depth of each line using a gauge; for example, mark the desired depth of each line on a toothpick. Insert the toothpick into the incision to see if you need to remove additional wood. Remember, it is best to go over the same line several times when removing wood, rather than making deep gouges that ruin the piece.

Project: Grab the Bull by the Horns

A bull design is a fantastic starting point when you want to practice the incised technique. The back and legs have longer strokes while the head, shoulders, and other areas have curves, so you can practice both grips in one piece. For this design, use a 10" x 6" x ½" piece of softwood, such as balsa or basswood. Do an internet search to find a picture of a bull and print it out to fit the piece of wood. You only want an outline, so select an image (called a pattern) that has long and curved lines but not too much detail. Let's get started:

1. Transfer the bull image to your piece of wood by drawing over the printout with a ballpoint pen. A light, indented design should be visible on the wood once you remove the paper. You might want to go over these lines with a pencil to see more clearly. Alternatively, use carbon paper while tracing the design. Just keep in mind that pencil and carbon marks may change the color of the wood, so you have to remove that with light sanding later on.

2. Using your tool of choice, start from the bull's shoulders and make a long stroke for the back. A low grip helps in maintaining a consistent depth. Make any additional long cuts wherever it is suitable for your design.

3. Change to a high grip and start working on incising the outline of the head, hooves, and other elements. Try to incise an eye using a rounding action.

4. Check the depth of your cuts continuously during the process. Go over any lines that require extra depth until the entire piece is complete.

Use only one tool the first time you make this design so that you get to know its grips and cuts. Once you are done with this project, repeat the process with a new tool but using the same image. You can do this as many times as you want and even try a combination of tools. It creates a great visual comparison for referencing and learning the difference between the tools.

Think about your finished product before you start incise carving. Usually, either the incised line or the background is accentuated in a contrasting color. If you want the background to be darker and the lines lighter, then you have to stain or varnish the wood and let it dry before you start carving. Alternatively, paint the incised lines once you are done carving.

Chip Carving

Chip carving is a decorative wood carving technique that has been around for centuries. Many gothic artworks, churches, doors, and trays feature intricately carved wood using chip carving. Usually, flat surfaces work best for this technique, although it is used to produce features such as eyes on rounded surfaces.

In its most basic form, chip carving requires several cuts from different angles and directions to remove a wood chip. Removing many wood chips reveals beautiful, ornamental designs. Cuts are made at an angle, which creates a bevel. The word "bevel" means angle or slant, indicating various depths within the design.

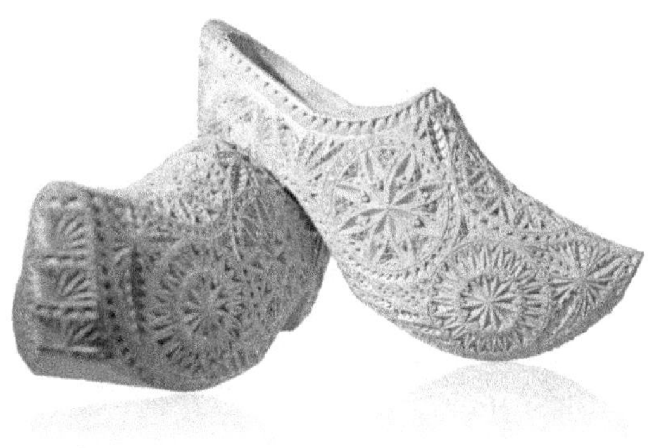

Chip carving is classified into two types that have distinct characteristics. The first type is fine triangle chip carving, which is exactly as the name says: removing triangular chips by following a pattern of lines. Fine triangle works well for intricate designs, such as flowers with a lot of detail, and to create consistent, repetitive designs. The second type is free-form chip carving. This method does not follow a specific pattern; rather, you make cutlines as you see fit from a suitable direction. Free-form works best in creating imaginative pieces, although most projects require a combination of these techniques.

Essential Tools

Various knives work best for chip carving. These knives include chip carving knives, stab knives, and detail knives. Your traditional pocket knife, flat blade, or raindrop razor edge work well, although you may want to invest in the additional tools as it makes chipping easier.

At some time, you are going to find that your knife cannot carve the chip you desire, usually because the wood is too hard. This is an indication that you should use a chisel and mallet for chip carving. A mallet is essential when wood becomes tough because you can remove chips more easily, while the chisel glides more easily through the wood. Use the chisel in a similar way as a knife but tap it lightly with the mallet so that it cuts into the wood.

Hand Positions

Chip carving requires specific hand positions during the carving process so that your design can come to life. These positions dictate your grip on the handle and the pivoting point, as removing chips necessitates a pivoting action.

- *Basic*: Hold the knife in a clenched hand with the top of the knife (where the blade meets the handle) resting on your index finger. Gently guide the tip of the blade into the wood at a 30 - 45 degree angle and use the handle as the pivot.

- *Straight wall*: The straight-wall position aims to create a cut that is almost perpendicular to the surface of the wood. Drive the blade into the wood using an 85 - 90 degree angle and focus on creating a deep cut. Usually, straight wall cuts are made along two sides of a triangle.

- *Curved edge*: Curves frequently appear in chip carving, especially when cutting flower petals or spiral designs. The key to the curved edge is changing the angle of your hand. Start at the tip of the pattern with the blade at a 45-degree angle. Decrease the angle to 30 degrees as you reach the center of the cut, then increase the angle after the middle so that it is back to 45 degrees by the time you reach the end. Think of this method in the same way as scooping food from a bowl.

- *Three or Four-sided*: Start by holding the knife in the basic position but use a 45-degree angle. Push the knife into one part of the shape at a time and press it towards the center of the shape.

- *Sloped floor to straight-wall*: This position requires a shallow cut that meets a straight wall (perpendicular) on one side. Use a knife with a flatter blade and hold it as flat as possible to the wood, almost horizontally, while pushing forward.

Practical Tips

Chip carving is not as challenging as it might seem and you have probably used some of these positions already. However, you can improve your skills by keeping a few things in mind while chip carving. Your hand position will make or break your cut so practice the method ahead of time. Do not rest your hand on the wood or table, as it changes the cutting angle. It is okay to rest your thumb on the table or wood since it creates a pivot point from which to work. Keep your wrist straight at all times to avoid changing your angle without your knowledge. Rather, move your knife from your elbow for consistent angles and smoother lines.

Chip carving is tiring on the hands. Many beginner carvers hold their knives too tight when chip carving because they think it gives better control. It is not the case and can cause you to cut too deeply, which ruins the piece. Your hands will hurt too, so keep a firm grip on the handle and stop if your hands start cramping. An ergonomic handle is advisable if you are going to hold a knife for a long time.

Many designs have repetitive patterns that require the same cuts to be made numerous times. It is best to cut the first side on all the shapes, then cut the second side, and then the first side. This method ensures uniformity among the design and makes it look more professional. Generally, chip carving requires one cut from each side to create the design. Cutting from the same side of a shape multiple times is not recommended as the angle and force may change the chip size, which creates an inconsistent result.

Ragged surfaces after chipping indicate one of two things. The wood may be too hard making it difficult for you to cut through in a swift motion. Using a mallet, apply a light force to the back of a chisel (not a knife), which makes it glide more easily and requires less strength from you. However, the more likely cause is a dull blade, so sharpen your tools properly and try again.

Project: Practice makes Perfect

A multitude of patterns and projects are available for chip carving. Truly, it is a wood carving technique that unleashes creativity because you can carve anything your heart desires. Before you start on intricate projects, you have to master the basic positions and cuts. Jumping into a specific pattern immediately might lead to disappointment if your cutting doesn't quite go to plan. So, start by practicing on a smooth, blank piece of wood. Clean a slab of butternut wood, about 12" x 10" x ½", to create a sampler board for practicing and grab your tools.

1. Draw parallel lines ½" apart across the length of the wood. Do the same along the width so that you are left with a grid.

2. Draw triangles in each block in the first row with the two rows below that forming larger triangles. Use the basic position to carve out one triangle in each block. Practice consistent cutting using the same angle for at least five blocks before changing the angle.

3. In the next available line use the four-sided position to cut a row of squares.

4. Draw half circles across the next row. Make a straight wall cut along the diameter of each circle. Next, carve out the half-circle using the curved edge position.

5. Over the next two rows, you can practice the sloped floor to straight-wall. Make a straight wall cut at the top of each

square and then use the length of the two rows to create the sloped floor.

6. Use the remaining section of the wood for free-form chip carving. Draw ovals, curved lines, or other shapes and carve each one by changing the cutting angle and direction.

Softwoods are the best option for chip carving because they contain less grain and cut away easily. Butternut or balsa is soft enough to chip with little effort. However, you can chip carve harder woods such as mahogany or white oak. Dense woods are difficult to use in chip carving, so you require a mallet and chisel for proper use.

Secret 4: Certain carving techniques perform better when combined with specific types of wood. Every woodcarver requires awareness of these winning carving combinations.

Chapter 2:
Intaglio and Relief Carving

By now, you probably realize that you have been using some of these techniques already. Whittling is such a versatile hobby that learning new techniques comes to a person with little effort. The next two techniques are intaglio and relief carving. These techniques differentiate clearly between the foreground (or design) and the background (the wood surface. The main difference between the two carving techniques is these two levels. With intaglio, you are carving the design into the wood but with relief carving, you remove the background to reveal the design. Both techniques use elements of incised and chip carving, so mastering them is possible.

Intaglio Carving

Intaglio is a carving technique where the carver cuts a design into the wood and hollows out areas to create an image. It is similar to engraving, incised carving, and chip carving but the main difference lies in the larger areas of wood being removed, rather than just a line or chip. In fact, chip carving is a type of intaglio carving. The main design extends into the wood while the surface of the wood remains the background and at a higher level than the design. Some people call this reverse carving or negative relief carving, however, this book uses the traditional term, intaglio.

Intaglio carving is a popular technique for paneled items, like jewelry boxes, doors, and tabletops. Another use for intaglio is seen in furniture and moldings, where cutting into the work creates curves and crevices, like those often seen at the foot of a chair. Intaglio is the perfect technique if your finished piece will be used frequently because it will not chip away at the design, even if the raised surface experiences some damage. Patterned rolling pins, wax sealing stamps, and cookie presses all utilize the intaglio technique in the final product.

Essential Tools

Intaglio carving does not require specialized tools, although you may want to invest in additional gouges. Traditional whittling knives have flatter blades, except for hook knives that create curvature. Whittling knives can be used for intaglio but the artwork then requires a lot more cuts and producing consistent curvature becomes a challenge. It is much better to purchase gouges, which are used for other techniques too. Both u-shape and v-shape gouges are a valuable addition to your wood carving equipment.

Intaglio Carving Fundamentals

Seven cuts are fundamental for intaglio carving. Practice each cut before you start working on a project so that you understand the technique and create precise carvings. None of these methods are difficult but they do require some practice. It is also a good idea to make a practice board for yourself that shows each fundamental cut clearly for future reference. Hold your tool in a similar position as the basic cut for chip carving and keep the blade at a 30- to 45-degree angle to the wood.

Single Pass Trough

Measure the width of the gouge then draw two lines on a segment of wood, which are narrower than the gouge. Start at one end and place the gouge's edge between the two lines. Using a consistent force, push the gouge along the wood to create a trough-type shape. A u-shaped gouge creates a circular trough while the v-gouge produces a v-cut.

Double Pass Center Ridge

A ridge is a raised area between two troughs. Create a ridge by drawing three parallel lines instead of two. Next, create a single pass trough between the first two lines, then make a single pass trough between the next two lines. The line in the middle should remain raised to form the ridge. Creating this ridge requires a precise hand for maximum straightness and effect.

Square-Sided Trough

Sometimes, you want a trough with clear cut sides and a more angular design. A square-sided trough has well-defined sides that meet in a deeper v-cut. For this technique, you require a v-gouge that is narrower than the trough you are carving. Start by drawing parallel lines wider than the gouge. The square-sided trough requires multiple passes, so carve the left side, then the right, and finally the middle. Place the "v" of the gouge on the left line and angle the blade so that it is square along the line. Use a smooth stroke to carve the left edge of the trough. Repeat the process to create the right edge of the trough. Next, carve the middle of the trough by placing the v-gouge upright, producing a definite corner within the trough.

Single Pass Ellipse

Draw an ellipse with the widest part being smaller than the gouge. Place the blade at the edge of the ellipse and cut lightly into the wood. Increase the pressure slightly while following the two lines on the sides of the gouge so that the cut widens. Lighten the pressure when you pass the middle so that you can carve the ellipse smaller towards its rounded edge. Reaching the end of the ellipse may create a long chip that obscures the drawn lines, so you might want to break off the chip and then continue carving for a precise rounding.

Multiple Pass Ellipse

This technique is necessary when the ellipse is wider than the gouge. Start by making a trough-type cut along the middle of the ellipse. Next, place the blade on the left-side line and follow the line to make the next pass. Keep a consistent angle so that the cut lines up with the previous one. Repeat this process on the other side to create a complete ellipse.

Depending on the size of the ellipse, you may require more passes.

Cup

A cup shape is a great option when you want to create only part of an ellipse. Think of it as half of an ellipse, or a half-circle. Draw an ellipse half and close off the opening with a straight line. Make the cut with a gouge using the single-pass ellipse technique but stop at the straight edge. Use a straight blade knife and cut along the straight line to stop the cut, then remove the chip.

Globe Cut

Although ellipses are great, there are times when you want a perfect circle or globe shape, like when you create eyes in a carving. Make a circle on your wood by placing the edge of the gouge perpendicular to the surface and rotate it around its axis - you should be left with a perfect circle. Do not press too hard, as you just want the basic shape. Next, angle your blade for the depth you want and pass it around the circle several times until a round wood chip comes loose from the center. Scoop out this piece, then smooth out the globe by making additional passes. A round incision should have shadows on the inside due to the depth.

Project: Sailing the Seas

Intaglio carving projects can be intricate with multiple designs or simple scenes. If you are carving a scene, then the elements closest to the forefront has to be carved the deepest. Aspects that are further into the background will be shallow or not carved at all since intaglio is a reverse carving technique. Any softwood measuring 8" x 6" x 1/" works for this project.

1. Draw a sailing scene onto the wood. Start by drawing a shoreline in the lower quarter of the wood, then add some sand dunes or mountains slightly above that. Draw a sailboat in the middle of the block so that it meets the shoreline. The picture can be as easy or difficult as you like but include at least two sails. The front of the sailboat should point towards the left edge of the piece of wood.

2. The item furthest away from the viewer is the land between the shore and sky, so start your intaglio design by carving

away between these two lines using a wide gouge. Only remove the top layer of the wood.

3. Use a very thin gouge to emphasize the shoreline by cutting a slightly deeper trough. Next, give texture to the water by removing a thin layer of wood using a wide gouge. Vary the depth of your cuts to create the effect of moving water.

4. Redraw the boat on your wood; if some of it has been shaved off then start carving the deck of the sailboat. The bowline should be left intact but use a thin gouge to remove enough wood from the hull. Make deeper cuts towards the front of the boat as it is closer to the viewer. Add a deep v-cut where the waterline meets the boat.

5. Carve a deep angled outline around the left-side sail, then use different size gouges to create depth in the sail. Do the same with the right-hand sail but make the carving slightly shallower, as it is further into the background.

6. Make a v-cut mast using a thin gouge or veiner.

7. Add any other details you want to the scene. Try making a globe cut sun or adding trees in the background. Once you are done, sand the piece and finish it according to your preferences.

Relief Carving

Relief carving is a technique whereby a thick slab of wood is carved to reveal a three-dimensional scene with a flat background. It is the opposite technique to intaglio that creates an image towards the inside of the wood. The final design of relief carving generates a protruding scene, which produces an illusion of dimension through shadows. Relief carving is one of the most beautiful techniques that most woodcarvers want to master. Ancient Egypt and Greece produced many relief carving masterpieces that depict the history of the nation.

There are several relief styles that a carver can choose between to produce an artwork. *High relief* pieces create dramatic visuals as the piece is carved with a depth of ½" to 2", which takes an extremely long time to carve. A variation of this style is *deep relief carving* where the carving is deeper than 2", but you need a wood slab that is double that thickness to avoid warping. *Low relief* pieces have a depth of less than ½" making it a trickier carve as lots of details have to go into a shallower design. One technique used in low relief (sometimes called bas) is leveling, such as when a flower is in front of a leaf. Pierced relief carving is an intricate style where small holes are pierced through the wood to create additional visual depth.

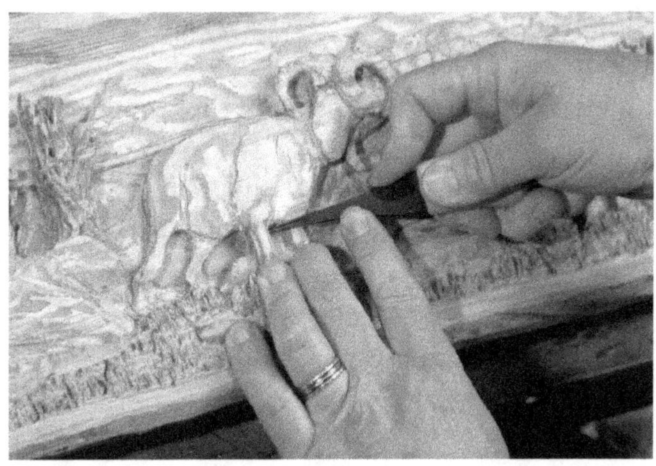

All relief carving pieces have distinct stages to complete the artwork. First, prepare a suitable slab of wood by sanding and cleaning the surface. Second, obtain a pattern or draw one yourself and transfer it onto the panel. Third, outline the main design by making incised cuts around key features and removing some of the surrounding wood. Fourth, remove any unwanted background material or enhance the areas around your main projects by deepening the cuts. Next, model the main design by adding additional features in finer detail. Finally, tidy up the background by removing any additional wood, if necessary, and apply a suitable finish.

Essential Tools

Chisels, gouges, and mallets are the main tools necessary for relief carving. The wider your range of tools, the more detail you can add to your artwork, so try to add equipment when possible. Additionally, a variety of tools makes carving easier and faster, as you do not have to go over the same area multiple times. A good rubber mallet is essential for carving deeper sections, as few people have enough power to drive a chisel through the wood on its own.

Secret Five: *Relief carving is not as difficult as other people may have told you... if you use the correct tools.*

The type of wood you use does affect your carving too. Any wood can work for relief carving, but let your design lead your choice. Softer woods like butternut, pine, and basswood remain popular options. However, relief carving seldom uses very long strokes due to the high level of detail, so you can select a harder wood. Keep in mind that harder woods are more challenging to carve and not suitable for beginner relief carvers. Mahogany or Black Ash is ideal if you want a challenge but these woods can chip and tear if you are not confident in your strokes.

Relief Cuts

Relief cutting is a technique that uses several cuts made by specific tools for a set purpose. There are three basic cuts, two technical cuts, and the v-cut. You can make the v-cut using either the traditional whittling method or use a veiner tool.

- *Back up chisel cut*: This basic cut is made by using the thin side of the chisel to add finer details.

- *Back down chisel cut*: Another basic cut, use the back, thicker part of the chisel to make a thicker cut into the wood.

- *Gouge cut*: The final basic cut is used to create round areas on the piece or shave excess wood from the background.

- *Undercut*: As a technical cut, the undercut features in high relief work and underneath the main feature. The viewer cannot see these cuts, but they add shadow and depth, which provides additional detail.

- *Stop cut*: This technical cut has the same purpose as other stop cuts: to end a cut. For relief carving, use a chisel to cut into the wood making a stopping point, and then carve towards this point.

Project: Alphabet

Relief carving may seem daunting at first but it becomes manageable once you start practicing. Start with a simple project where you can practice the basic stages of relief cutting but without too much detail. The alphabet, or a specific letter, in this case, is a great place to start. Use a 10" x 7" x ½" piece of softwood and keep your gouges, chisels, and mallet ready. Just as with incised carving, you may want to use a depth gauge for added precision.

1. Prepare your wood by ensuring it is clean then transfer a letter pattern to the wood. You can use any letter of your

choosing and try this project several times with other letters until you master the technique. If you want to go very basic, then start with the "I". However, I would suggest going for "B" or "P" as they contain roundings and internal relief carving.

2. Turn the wood onto its side and mark a ⅓" all around the sides, so that you have a gauge for how deep you want to carve. For this letter, you will keep the letter raised from the wood and carve away everything along the outside, so markings on the side can assist in estimating depth.

3. Define the edge of the letter by making v-cuts using a low-angle grip just outside of the outline. This process acts as a stop cut for the letter and is sometimes called lining in.

4. Remove excess background material by using a gouge and making long strokes. Move from the edge of the wood towards the letter as it requires more control, but do not let the knife hit the letter. You want to remove all the wood up to the

marking line that was made around the wood in step 2.

5. Focus on the tighter and internal areas next. Remove the wood inside the loop of the letter but work carefully so that you do not ruin your piece. Always work towards the v-cut but never remove material that is lower than the stop cut.

6. Place a flat or rounded chisel (depending on the outline) onto the outline at the top left of the letter. Hit the tool lightly with the mallet, so that it forms a crisp cut that ends in the stopping cut. Do this all around the letter paying particular attention to defining corners and curves.

7. Smooth the edge of the letter by running a flat chisel or blade around while applying consistent pressure and remove any stray wood chips.

8. Finish the background by using flatter chisels in a low grip to remove any ridges. Sand the letter to ensure it is smooth and equalize the background. Apply a wax, varnish, or other finish.

There you have it - four techniques to add to your wood carving skill set. After practicing these four techniques, you can call yourself an intermediate whittler with a range of abilities and new projects begging for your attention. These extra techniques make it possible to create more elaborate pieces regardless of whether you carve for fun or for a side income. I think it is a great idea to sell some of your pieces, as you cannot keep all your work and it generates an income to buy new tools!

Chapter 3:
Upgrade Your Tools

The basic carving techniques do not require a lot of tools. For whittling, there are four main types of knives, namely, a pocket knife, a flat steel blade, a hook knife, and the raindrop razor edge. However, having additional tools makes wood carving easier and we already saw that some woodcarving techniques require other tools.

None of the tools mentioned in this chapter are specialized tools, since they apply to almost all wood carving techniques. Having the right tool not only makes carving easier but also places less pressure on your hands. Take some time to practice with a variety of tools and identify where they hurt you. Wrap some leather around those sections or use an ergonomic handle so that you can work comfortably.

- ***Secret Six***: *Ensure you hold and handle tools in the right way, especially carving knives. A grip that is too tight is just as dangerous and damaging as a grip that is too loose.*

The basic wood carving tool is a knife. Most people start with a simple pocket knife for whittling and later purchase additional knives for detail work or for hollowing out items such as spoons. A flat-bladed knife works well for making broad strokes but a detail knife with a thin taper, like a raindrop razor edge, makes it easier to add definition to your carving. Yet, new techniques may necessitate additional knives.

Chip Carving Knives

Chip carving requires a different type of knife than other techniques. Specifically, you need a chip carving knife created especially for this purpose. A chip carving knife has a shorter blade, often made from durable carbon steel, with an ergonomic grip to reduce strain on your hands and wrists. The blades are thin making it easier to cut into the wood and create precision cuts into corners or at different angles.

Chip carving knives are available as single units or as a set and most are priced reasonably. If this is your first purchase, then save up for a set of knives (usually three per pack) that offer a variety of blades. Popular blade shapes include an angled flat steel blade that works well for straight wall cuts, blades with a rounded back for shaping more easily, and blades that end in a thin, sharp point making it easier to cut into the corners or make triangular cuts.

Some carvers believe that whittling should only be done with a pocket knife but it is not the case with chip carving. A chip carving knife is a recommendation for this technique because the blade of pocket knives are too thick and have a rounder nose. Additionally, a pocket knife's blade is weaker than the blade of a chip carving knife and there is a risk that you could snap your pocket knife. Although a pocket knife is useful and can work for chip carving, the correct knife produces better results.

Stab Knives

A stab knife is necessary for straight lines and accents. The blade has an extremely sharp, straight edge that glides into the wood without much effort. Usually, a stab knife has an angled blade of about 45 degrees that assists in creating depth. Place the blade of the stab knife perpendicular to the wood and push it into the piece. Control your knife carefully; it is not necessary to stab the wood with force.

Stab knives come in many materials. Most blades are made from stainless or carbon steel, while the handles are either wood or resin. Some stab knives have notches on the handle, which helps you remember how you held the knife for a specific cut. Since most of the blade cuts into the wood at once, the blade must be kept sharp at all times.

Detail Knives

The name of this knife explains its intended purpose. Detail knives are used to add fine details and definition to the artwork. Most detail knives have a sharp pointed end to get into all the little corners of the cut. Use this knife to sharpen the features of a chip cut, intaglio design, and especially, to carve features using the relief carving technique.

Detail knives come in a variety of shapes and sizes so choose one that works for your application. Many people have a few detail knives, such as the basic raindrop razor edge for a start. A short blade reduces the distance between your hand and the wood, which gives greater control and accurate carving. However, a longer blade may help if you have a deeper cut that requires detailing.

Hook Knives

Carving straight edges is quite a straightforward exercise, but hollowing out wood with a straight blade is a major challenge. Luckily, hook knives save the day and make it easier to hollow out spoons, bowls, and other designs. A hook knife looks exactly as the name suggests: the blade is curved into the shape of a hook. Most whittlers own at least one hook knife, as it is an invaluable tool.

A wide variety of hook knives are available on the market. Select your hook knife carefully because the cheaper ones usually do not last long. Yet, many woodcarvers want more than one hook knife, as the blades differ in many ways. The curvature of the hook can be narrow or wide. A narrow hook produces smaller shavings, while the wider hooks have a greater surface area to create shallow cuts. The hook may end in a sharp point for deep cutting or have a flat edge that generates a rounder effect. Additionally, the blade of the hook knife can be sharp on one side or both. With this range of features, it makes it challenging to choose just one. A great strategy for increasing your hook knife collection is to purchase the knife only if your project requires one.

Chisels

Hardwoods, deep relief cutting, and chip carving may benefit from the use of chisels. A chisel is a steel rod with a differentiating tip for various purposes. Chipping wood and removing small shavings at angles are the main use for chisels, which make them a standard part of the wood worker's toolbox. Some chisels come with a definitive handle or have a handle that fits several separate tools. However, some chisels consist of only the steel shaft and have no ergonomic handle in any fashion.

The lack of handle and thicker blade makes it difficult to use just your own force to create a cut. Rather, the chisel is placed into the correct position and then hit with a mallet at the end of the shaft, which catapults the chisel into the wood. Chisels have many purposes besides word work and may be used in carving other materials or in DIY and building activities. Ensure your chisels are suitable for woodwork and keep your wood chisels separate from other tools so that you do not ruin the blade through improper use. Besides the chisels listed below, there are other shapes such as tooth and point chisels.

Flat Chisel

A flat chisel has a 6" to 10" shaft that ends in a sharp, flat edge. The perpendicular cutting edge is suitable for creating straight lines, such as borders. The flat cutting edge can vary in length with some as narrow as ⅛" and others widening to 4". Check that your chisel has a sharpened edge that creates a bevel, otherwise it might not cut into the wood.

Hold a flat chisel perpendicular to the wood for a definite stop cut or place it at an angle for a v-cut. This shape assists in creating curves, shaping the basic outline, and removing excess wood. A flat chisel leaves very few ridges when used correctly, so work carefully and save time.

Skew Chisel

The skew chisel has a slanted blade rather than a flat edge. The blades are available at various angles, which makes for deeper or shallower carving. It works well for chip and relief carving where the depth of the incision varies across the cut. The toe is the longest part of the angled blade, while the shorter section is known as a heel. Be careful when using a skew chisel as the toe can lodge deeper into the wood than the heel making it difficult to remove the chisel once being hit with a mallet.

Fishtail Chisel

A fishtail chisel is a type of flat chisel but the end shape is slightly different. The edge of the blade flares out towards both sides, which creates a shape going from thin at the base of the shaft to wide at the cutting edge. The fishtail shape makes it easier to work in small spaces as you can maneuver the chisel into the correct area and angle.

__Secret Seven__: Learn about the gouges of your chisels. The gouge represents the shape and size of your chisel blade. Do not confuse a chisel with a gouging tool. Ultimately, the blade's size and curvature matter a lot, as they determine the structure of the cut.

Gouges

A gouge tool removes slivers of woods and small clumps in hard to reach areas. Do not confuse a gouge with a gauge. A gouge is a cutting tool, while a gauge is a measuring tool. Gouges look like a combination between a knife and a chisel. Most people consider a gouge to be a chisel with a thin, curved blade and secure handle. Many gouge tools can be used just by applying force from your body; however, a light mallet tap can assist the blade if the wood is very hard.

Three Basic Cuts

Gouges and knives make similar cuts in wood. Yet, there are times that a knife doesn't do a cut justice and you need a better tool. Oftentimes, a gouge is a more versatile choice. Three basic cuts set gouge tools apart from knives and make them with the extra expense.

The first type makes a channel in the shape of a concave cut. Secondly, turning the blade 180 degrees allows you to make a convex cut with rounded wood at the top of the cut. Finally, gouges make plunge cuts when the gouge is pushed into the wood in an effort to make a stop cut (Ellenwood, 2008, p. 121). Achieving these shapes with a knife is challenging, takes a lot of time, and you have no guarantee that you will achieve the desired effect. Investing in gouges is a sensible choice, so look for a durable set with a variety of tools.

Size and Sweep

Manufacturers use the terms *size* and *sweep* to differentiate between gouges. The size of the blade is found by measuring the gouge across its width. Measure the blade at its widest part, but note that gouge' sizes are mostly given in metric units rather than inches. Check your set carefully to see which system was used by the manufacturer. Gouges come in many sizes from ⅛" to 1" providing several options for your carving.

The sweep of a gouge refers to curvature in the blade. Although there are slight variations between manufacturers, the definition of the sweep remains the same. A number (#) designates the sweep and ranges from #2 to #11, where a higher number indicates a deeper curve. Shallow gouges range between #2 and #4, medium-depth gouges are #5 to #7, deep gages include while #8 and #9. The deepest gouges are #10 and #11 and create thin, deep lines, similar to those made by veiners.

Clearly, there are many gouge tools when considering the sweep and size combinations. Yet, you do not need one in every size and depth. Purchase a thin and wider gouge within each sweep category as an initial set, then buy additional gouges when you can. Although size matters, the sweep is not precise, so there is leeway when following design instructions. For example, a #6 or #8 tool is suitable if the project requires a #8 gouge.

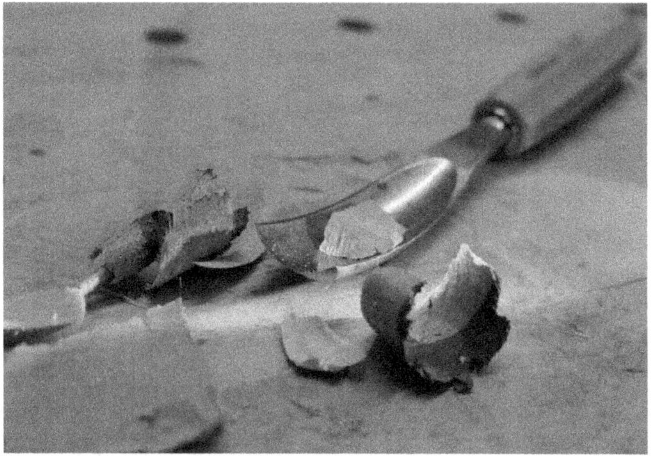

Spoon Gouge

A spoon gouge looks like a combination of a gouge and a hook knife. The general shape is similar to a spoon, which makes it easier to create a hollow in the wood. The curve at the end of the gouge is very short and tapers to a sharp blade so that you can get into tight corners. Additionally, turning the gouge around allows you to cut into the wood at an almost perpendicular angle.

V-Type Gouge

V-type gouges have an angled blade creating a "v" rather than a fluid curve. The size of the tool is measured as the widest part between the two edges, which are called wings in wood carving terms. Rather than having a numbered sweep, a v-tool comes with a specific angle made by the two blades. The most common v-tools have 45, 60, or 90-degree angles, although there are other options. A unique extension of this tool is a winged-v gouge that cuts a "v" while creating convex roundings along the side.

U-Type

A u-type gouge produces a trough with deeper sides than the traditional gouges. It is quite easy to confuse the two since the shapes are similar. U-type gouges are essential when making deep relief carving pieces, as you can remove more wood in less time. The shape is much more of an ellipse than a circle, so do not use this gouge for globe cuts.

Veiners

Veiners cut thin channels into the wood, just like the veins in your body. Use a veiner for fine details and features, such as deep cuts, outlines, and hair. Some confusion exists regarding veiners because they look a lot like gouges; however, there is no strict definition in this regard. A #11 gouge is the same size as a veiner. When comparing a #10 gouge with a veiner, you will see the wings of the veiner are higher making the cuts deeper than a gouge tool (Ellenwood, 2008, p. 122). Still, most people refer to this tool as a veiner, as it is easier to know what a person is talking about. A #11 veiner is an essential tool for all intermediate woodcarvers.

V-Tools

The v-tool, also known as a parting tool, has a blade with a distinct "v" shape for angular cutting. A v-tool helps in making outlines, undercuts, texture, and unique details. Some people believe that joining two chisel blades creates the v-tool but it is more complex than this simple definition. The difference between a v-tool and a v-gouge is the shape of the cut. The v-gouge creates a valley since it has a slight curvature in the sides, while the shape of the v-tools produces a wall as the blades are straight. V-tools come in various angles with the most popular options being 30, 45, 60, and 90 degrees. The smaller the angle between the blades, the thinner the line, so some manufacturers offer 24-degree v-tools for super fine lines.

Intermediate wood carving techniques require additional tools since you are expanding your skillset from just whittling. Build up your tool collection slowly and only purchase a tool if you need it for a project. Keep your tools in good condition by cleaning them thoroughly after every use. Sharpen the blades and store the tools properly, so that they last for a long time. Besides these tools, you might consider adding extra accessories to your workshop.

Chapter 4:
Accessorize Your Workshop

Accessories and other tools add value to your workshop and make your work a breeze. The tools in this chapter are not primary wood carving tools but some of them are useful in woodworking and improve the carving process. You might have these tools in your collection already or make purchases as you need the tools.

Secret Eight: *Hobbycraft stores create the perception that you need an abundance of tools when carving a masterpiece. But, you don't. A select few essentials will suffice, but you might carve more easily with some optional tools. Everything you need is specified in this book.*

Carving Mallet

Carving mallets are essential when working with chisels and sometimes for gouges, as they provide the force to move the tool through the wood. Mallets stocked at hardware stores come in a variety of shapes, sizes, and materials including metal, wood, and rubber. Metal and heavy mallets are not ideal for woodwork as their hardness may damage the tool you are hitting. A wood or light rubber mallet is preferable for carving, although some hobby shops stock mallets made for woodworking specifically. Some people turn their own wooden mallets from wood, which is a nice project for yourself, or ask a friend with a lathe to make one for you.

Mallets assist in moving tools through a medium, in this case, wood. The advantage of mallets lies in the strength with which you swing it, which gives great control. The harder you strike the complementary tool, the deeper the tool drives into the wood, while hitting it softer generates less movement. Always clamp the wood to a workbench when using a mallet, as the force can move the wood across the table (Ellenwood, 2008, p. 162).

Secret Nine*: Ensure you use a light mallet (or hammer) as much as possible. Using a heavier mallet can cause muscle strain, especially when using them improperly or if you do not know the basic technique. Never swing the mallet from your elbow; always use a swinging action coming from your shoulder.*

There are many types of woodworking mallets, so select one (or several) suitable for your intentions. A bench mallet is a large tool made from wood with angled sides that work well for driving tools into stubborn wood. The flatter sides on the width of the bench mallet work well when you require less pressure. A less familiar option is the carver's mallet that comes in three sizes and a variety of applications. The carver's mallet is unique as it does not have an angular head but has a distinctive bell-like shape. Use a larger carver's mallet with a chisel or gouge to remove a lot of background material without experiencing fatigue, or select a smaller one for light, precision work. Another variation is a brass carver's mallet, which has a wooden handle and a small, brass head. This mallet is ideal for precision carving with more weight and in small spaces.

Files

Files are a controversial tool in the wood carving community as purists believe these tools provide artificial finishing. However, modern carvers may find files as a useful accessory to finish work, especially when you want a smooth surface rather than ridges or textures. Files help in shaping the wood and smoothing the surface by removing small slivers and stray pieces. Using files for initial rough finishing often works faster than using sandpaper, although you still need to sand your piece for a pristine finish.

Each file has three distinct parts, namely, the length, tang, and heel. The file's length is the cutting area, which has teeth on it for filing. Larger teeth create a coarser surface while smaller, closely packed teeth make for a finer filing surface. The smoother and slightly tapering section between the length and tang is called the heel. The tang is an area at the end of the file, which is usually tapering and thinner. Note that a handle must be placed over the tang, as it is not a handle in itself. Most files come without a handle since one interchangeable handle can be used for all files.

File types are a reference to the cutting surface of the file and determine the abrasiveness. Use a single-cut file for precision work. A double-cut and coarse file removes wood quickly, while bastard and second files remove less wood and at a slower pace. The smooth type removes wood very slowly and leaves a smooth surface, which is ready for sanding.

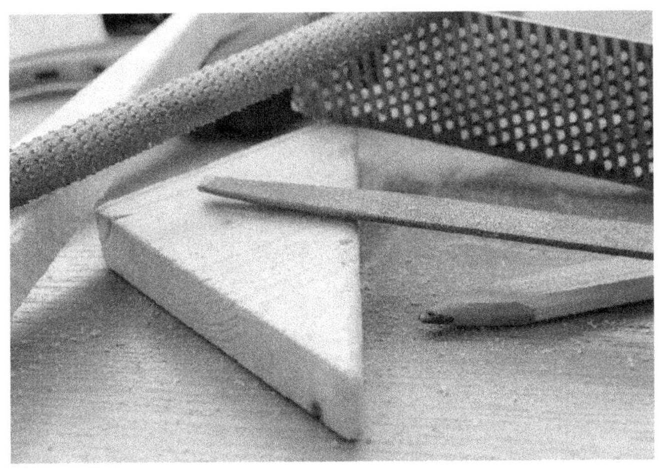

There are many file shapes called profiles. Each one has a specific application but you do not need a file of every type and size. The profile, or shape of the length, determines the use of the file. Basic file profiles include rectangular, semi-circle, triangular, round, square, and tapered shapes that fit into a variety of spaces. Remember that files can clog with frequent use and become dirty, so clean them after use with a nylon brush. Store them away from moisture to avoid damage and apply chalk before use to discourage clogging.

Rasps

A rasp is a very coarse type of file that removes wood quickly. Rather than planing the surface, rasps scrape away at the top layer and leave a rough surface for further finishing. The length of a rasp contains triangular teeth, arranged randomly for faster working. The larger sized teeth prevent clogging as wood slivers fall out while using a rasp. A smaller variety of rasps exists because they are not used for precision work.

Needle Files

Needle files are thin, smaller sized files, which come in many profiles. These files are the right tool for precise filing and have a second cut surface for a smoother finish. Most hardware and hobby craft stores sell needle files in a set of twelve with an interchangeable handle.

Rifflers

Rifflers are smaller files but have a file length on both ends in different sizes. It does not have a handle but the middle section of the file has an area for easier gripping. The filing ends are available in several profiles with most tools having the same profile on both ends although one side will be smaller than the other. Popular shapes include knife, round, curve, triangle, square, and straight ends, among others. Rifflers can fit into tight working areas, which make them ideal for relief work.

Microplanes

A microplane is a very coarse file, similar to a cheese grater's finest place. Microplanes have curved or flat blades and contain small holes throughout the length to remove wood slivers rapidly. Be careful when using a microplane as you can hurt yourself easily. Microplanes are ideal for removing large areas of wood stock like backgrounds in relief carving.

Filing Styles

Many people just grab a file and get going but filing incorrectly can damage the wood and ruin your hard work. Use one of the following two styles for filing to finish your work properly. These filing styles assist in treating the wood properly and makes final finishing easier.

The first style is draw filing to finish a piece. Hold the handle with one hand and the tip of the file with the other hand and place the file perpendicular to the wood. Push the file across the wood surface using very little pressure. Too much pressure may remove wood excessively and create additional hollow areas. The teeth only file on the forward, pushing stroke, so remove the file from the wood surface and start again, rather than pulling it back across the wood.

Cross filing is the second style and helps in removing rougher areas of wood. Place the file at an angle to the wood while holding both ends of the file and run it across the wood with medium pressure. Never place the file flat and straight across the wood as it has too much friction. Insufficient pressure results in the file skipping over the wood causing irreparable damage. Always use a diagonal stroke when filing across the grain to avoid wood tears and splitting.

Clamping Devices

In whittling, you hold the wood with your hands and sometimes support it against another surface. The new techniques require you to use both hands while carving, such as holding a chisel in one hand and a mallet in the other, making it difficult to keep the wood stable. A piece of wood moving across the table (sometimes called walking) is detrimental and can ruin your piece entirely. However, the force applied is highly likely to move the wood, so you need to hold it in place with some type of clamp.

There are many types of clamps so find some that work for you and the project you are working on. An oddly-shaped project and the hardness of the wood determine the best clamp for the job as you have to secure it properly without damaging the wood. Clamps also assist in holding wood pieces together when you create joins or add glued elements onto the wood.

Carver's Vise

A vise is a holding tool that attaches to the workbench for extra stability. Vises move along several dimensions, although traditional workshop vises only have two plates that move apart. A carver's vise has additional clamping areas to ensure a piece is properly secured for carving. The best vise option is one that moves in all three dimensions as you have a wider range of clamping options. Do some research before purchasing a carver's vise, as you want one that clasps properly and has a gripping mounting plate. The vise and wood being held should not slip even when using a mallet.

Carver's Arm

The carver's arm is an extension of the vise and provides additional mobility for woodcarvers. The tool looks like a human arm and has a hinge joint that bends in the direction you want, which is usually up and down positions. Some carver's arms include a separate screw at the arm's end for side-to-side movement. The vertical and horizontal movement makes the carver's arm a desirable tool that eases the strain on the hands. Maple wood is a popular choice for carver's arms as it is strong and does not hurt the piece it is holding. Although carver's arms are reasonably priced, you can find instructions online to make your own one.

Machinist's Vise

A machinist's vise is the traditional workbench vise with a set of jaws that can be opened and closed along a set range. The plates on the inside of the jaw are metal and may have serrated areas, which may damage the wood while clamping. However, you want to secure the wood properly to avoid slippage when hitting a tool with a mallet. The best way to protect your wood and secure it tightly is to place a piece of softwood on each side of your work so that the vise's plates press against the spare blocks rather than directly against the carving piece. Alternatively, some hardware and woodcraft stores sell protective pads that attach to the plates by a magnet and provide cushioning for the wood being held.

Alligator Clips

An alligator clip is a long, pointed clamp that looks similar to an alligator's jaw and has a few serrated teeth. These clips are used for more than just wood and are often found at the end of cables, such as those at the end of vehicle jump-starting cables. However, alligator clips are a lot smaller and come in various sizes so you can select clips that fit your piece. Keep in mind that the serrated jaw may bite into the wood, especially softwoods, so attach the clips in areas that will be finished or removed later on. Many carvers secure alligator clips to rods and a table weight, which enables the piece to be held midair and makes it easier to work all around. Alligator clips can slip so secure them properly and do not use force on the wood as it can dislodge the piece.

Web Clamp

A web clamp is made by wrapping a ratchet strap around the wood. A ratchet strap, made from nylon, has a ratchet end that pulls the strap taut and keeps the piece together tightly. Ratchet straps are mainly used for joining pieces of wood or holding glued elements onto the wood so that they attach properly. A web clamp is effective and easy to use but has a lot more strength than you may think once pulled taut. Never place the ratchet area directly against the wood as it can scratch away at the surface; rather, keep it in the open area of the web. Additionally, check that the straps do not cut into the wood and cause unnecessary damage. Add a small block of softwood between the nylon strap and working piece for additional protection but check that the block does not slip while tightening the ratchet strap.

Rubber Bands

Rubber bands work well to hold wood that has odd shapes. Most clamping devices are made to hold wood pieces that are of a particular size or shape, usually with flat or rectangular surfaces. However, many whittling and wood carving pieces are not angular at all and have three-dimensional objects or rounded edges. Clamping these pieces in traditional clamps is very challenging and an item that slips can experience damage that ruins your hard work. In these cases, rubber bands are the best options as they hold the wood securely even when it is a strange shape. Opt for a wider rubber band that won't cut into the pieces instead of thin office-type rubber bands. Check that the rubber bands are in good condition before using them and discard any band that has cracks or dry spots as they may snap while holding the piece.

C, Spring, Quick-Change, and Toggle Clamps

A variety of shaped clamps holds wood to a workbench or assists in joining pieces of wood together. These clamps get their names from their shape or clamping mechanism. Many types exist, and these four are some of the most popular options, but you can use any type that you prefer or have available in your workshop.

C-clamps secure wood panels to the workbench so that it does not move during the carving process. Sizes range between 1" and 12" so use clamps that correspond to the size of your work. Using a too large clamp makes it prone to movement or slipping when pushed by hand while a clamp that is too small cannot hold the piece securely. C-clamps require manual manipulation to open and close, and tightening them can be a time-consuming process, especially when you need to clamp the work quickly.

A spring clamp is an automatic clamp that opens and closes quickly. The tips pressing against the wood and handles have a polyvinyl coating to decrease the chance of damage. A variety of sizes are available including mini-clamps and larger options up to 4". Spring clamps are especially useful when you need to create a good bond between glued objects as they apply sufficient pressure on the items.

Another alternative is the quick-change clamp that has a user-friendly mechanism. Slide the jaws onto the sides of the wood then tighten the grip by squeezing the pistol. A trigger releases the jaws when you are ready to remove the wood. All of these actions can be done by using only one hand, so a quick change clamp is perfect when you have to hold onto the wood while grabbing a clamp quickly. The jaws of quick-change clamps usually have a soft coating for added protection. However, the pressure applied by the jaws is not strong enough to glue pieces of wood together and the wood may move if you apply a heavier mallet blow.

Toggle clamps are another option for holding projects. These clamps have a lever handle and rubber tip that locks the wood into place. The rubber coating protects the wood from damage, but the clamp might be in your way while working on the piece. Attaching the clamp to the wood is easy, as you only need to pull the handle up or push it down and it secures itself.

Bar and Pipe Clamps

Bar and pipe clamps have been around for generations to hold longer objects securely. Most consist of a long shaft that has a fixed head and a tail that slides along the device. Traditionally, a bar clamp has a rectangular steel shaft to which the head and tail connects, although there are some differences in design. A pipe clamp is similar but fits onto any length of ¾" threaded pipe. With a pipe clamp, the head is screwed into place while the tail slides along the pipe and has a disc clutch for holding purposes.

Bar and pipe clamps come in lengths ranging from 4" to 6 feet, so they are a versatile tool for holding small or large projects. Some of these clamps now feature fast action sections that secure the wood quickly and easily. Find an option that works best for the size of your design and check that the jaws do not damage the wood when clamping. These clamps are ideal when carving figurines, totem poles, and three-dimensional pieces.

Numerous tools and accessories can enhance your wood carving experience. These tools are not essential but make it easier to hold your pieces and assist in finishing projects beautifully. While these additional tools are a great extension to carving equipment, you also need proper wood to create a masterpiece.

Chapter 5:
Know Your Wood

Comprehensive knowledge of wood, grain, and its behavior empowers a carver to select a suitable blank and carve a masterpiece. The more you know, the better your work and ability to use the wood. The basic anatomy of wood includes the crown, trunk, and roots.

Secret Ten*: Understanding the anatomy of wood and knowing the best wood type for different techniques is more important than owning many high-tech carving tools.*

The crown includes all the branches, twigs, limbs, and leaves. Through photosynthesis, the leaves produce food for the rest of the tree, which is called sap and transported throughout the tree. The trunk is the segment in between the crown and roots, which often is a wide, solid area, free of limbs. The roots anchor the tree and absorb minerals and water from the ground. The trunk is of most importance to carvers since it contains the best carving wood.

Parts of a Tree Trunk

The tree trunk is the large, upright area of the tree. From the trunk grows branches that support flowers, fruit, and leaves. Five layers make up the trunk of all trees, starting from the outer bark and moving towards the heartwood, which is the deepest layer. Each layer has a specific role and affects the usability of the wood, so get to know it and your work becomes better.

Outer Bark

On the very outside of the tree is the outer bark, which protects the trunk from external elements. The outer bark renews itself from inside the trunk so that the tree does not dry out in the heat or absorb excess moisture when it rains. It also provides insulation to extreme weather conditions and prevents insects from entering the wood.

Inner Bark

Also known as phloem, the inner bark transports food between the inside and outside of the tree and the leaves. The inner bark has a short lifespan but works hard during that time.

Once it dies, the inner bark transforms into cork and changes to outer bark.

Cambium Cell Layer

The area below the inner bark is the cambium cell layer, which is the layer responsible for trunk growth. Responsible for new bark production, the cambium cell layer uses hormones, called auxins, from the inner bark to stimulate growth. Auxin production occurs when leaf buds start growing on tree branches, usually during Springtime.

The cambium cell layer, sometimes called sap, is the sticky liquid released from trees when they are cut. The time of year that a tree is cut determines the amount of liquid in the cell layer. During spring and summer, the cambium layer experiences rapid cell division making cuts very sticky and bark often fall from the tree as it does not have a good binding agent to the sapwood. During winter and fall, growth slows and fewer cells form in the cambium layer, which generates a tight bond between sapwood and bark. Some carving projects get aesthetic appeal when the bark remains intact during the carving process. If you want to try this method, then use a tree from a fall or winter harvest.

Sapwood

Sapwood is a softer and younger wood between the cambium cell layer and heartwood. The sapwood transports water from the roots to the branches and leaves. Sapwood fulfills this role for several years until it loses vitality when new rings are formed through growth. Sapwood has a lighter color than heartwood so it is easy to distinguish between the different layers.

Heartwood

Heartwood lies at the center (heart) of the tree and is the supporting structure for the rest of the tree. Technically, the heartwood is dead, but it remains strong and does not decay if the external layers are healthy. Heartwood is a composite material that contains hollow cellulose fibers held together by lignin, which is similar to glue. This composite material has exceptional strength and can support a lot of weight.

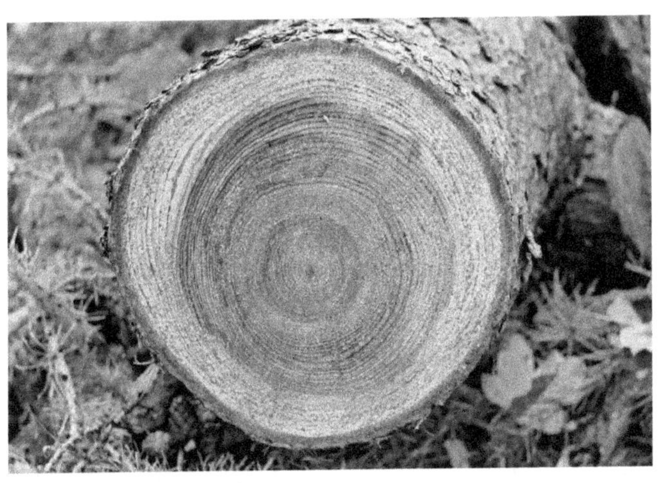

Understanding Wood Behavior

Besides the original five layers, wood has other characteristics that dictate its usability and behavior. The qualities are internal to the wood and cannot be seen without making a cross-section into the tree. However, these attributes are visible once the trunk is cut.

Pith

The pith is found right in the middle of the tree and becomes visible in the trunk. It is the oldest part of the tree and referred to as juvenile wood. The pith has some inherent weaknesses that cause it to crack easily, which may extend to the rest of the wood if it dries out or becomes vulnerable. Most carvers do not use the pith area in their work as it is brittle. If your wood does have a pith, then position the design to avoid the pith or keep it away from view.

Annual Rings

Annual rings are a growth indicator for trees that start around the pith and move all the way to the exterior of the wood. The rings contain two parts known as spring or earlywood, and summer or latewood. Active growth occurs during the growing season and forms the earlywood, which has thin walls and large cells. Growth decreases throughout the season, creating thicker walls with smaller cells, known as latewood. A higher concentration of cellulose gives latewood a darker color. These two parts create a definite ring for each year of growth with varying width dependent on growing conditions.

Vessels and Rays

Vessels and rays are the circulatory systems of trees that transport substances throughout the wood. Vessels run vertically through the tree and appear as small holes when a cross-section of wood is placed under a microscope. The vessels are responsible for transporting minerals and water from the roots to the leaves. Rays run horizontal to the tree and appear as lines under a microscope. During photosynthesis, the sap produced is sent to the rest of the wood through these rays. Vascular rays have thinner cell walls and weave around the vessels to bond them together.

Even though vessels and rays require a microscope to be seen properly, they have a big impact on wood behavior. Sometimes, a gouge or knife enters an area between vessels and tears the ray cells apart, which splits the vessels. This issue is known as "splitting with the grain" and creates tears in the wood. Cutting across the grain is a better option since you do not cut into the vessels. These potential problems emphasize the importance of grain familiarity with cutting.

Wood Grain

Wood grain is a term used to describe the appearance, texture, and alignment of wood fibers. Fibers are long thin cells that grow in a certain direction to create alignment with other cells. The grain is visible when you cut into the wood but you need additional information to use this identification for proper wood carving practices.

Grain texture refers to the cell arrangement, size, and variation, which create either fine or coarse grain. As the wood dries out, the vessels become empty and form pores, which are a distinguishing element between soft and hardwood. Softwood has densely packed fibers, while large pores in hardwood make them difficult to carve. Closed grain wood has very small pores that are difficult to see, while wood with large pores is known as open grain. Carving wood may be susceptible to tears if the pores are large.

The grain orientation creates a pattern known as figure grain, which is used in some projects. There are four types of grain patterns that are important for woodcarvers. A *straight grain* block of wood has a grain that runs in only one direction throughout the wood. When cell growth extends from the tree center, the pattern is known as *cross-grain*. Sometimes, a tree trunk twists over many years of growth, which creates a *spiral-grain*. Finally, *interlocked grain* patterns occur when twists in the trunk force fibers into different areas causing misalignment.

Figure grain has qualities that differentiate cuts and wood from each other because vessels and rays grew uniquely. *Silver grain* is seen when some types of trees are sawn in a specific way to reveal prominent rays. Using a wood cutting from a section where branches and limbs meet creates a *crotch figure*. Sometimes, the vessels have a wavy growth pattern referred to as *curly grain*. *Bird's eye* grain is seen when layers of cells cause small dimples in the wood, while larger dimples result in *quilted figure* grain. However, dimples occur when a fungal infection affects the tree. A *ribbon figure* is seen when vessels change their direction after a few years of growth. Finally, the *burl figure* represents grain that caused a growth on the side of the tree in a swirling pattern.

Grain plays a role in every single cut made into the wood. Knowing the types of grain and how it behaves when applying tools is essential. When a tool enters the wood at the wrong angle, it can damage the wood and split the layers. Sometimes, the tool then becomes stuck in the wood, and extracting it causes further damage, while the tool may slip at other times and cut into the wrong area.

Working With The Grain

The grain assists in determining the direction of a cut and gives you an idea of any issues that may pop up during the process. The most important thing is to cut across the grain so that you do not split the vessels. However, most books, hobby craft stores, and internet searches suggest cutting with the grain, but that is exactly when splits occur.

Secret Eleven: *A common belief among carvers is that carving should occur along (or with) the wood grain. Wood splitting often occurs when carving along the grain. However, carving across the grain is easier, as you have better control over the pieces of wood being removed from the work.*

Two-grain cutting styles have been mentioned already but there are other cutting methods too. Cutting *across the grain* refers to cuts made perpendicular to vessels, while parallel cuts are typical of cutting *with the grain*. Another option is to cut the wood at an angle to the grain, which is known as cutting *against the grain*. When a person does cut into the grain, they make incisions between the vessels. However, this cut easily produces *splitting with the grain*, which tears the wood (Ellenwood, 2008, p. 67). Although most projects come with instructions on the best grain and cut to use, there are many instances where the wood you have available necessitates other forms of cutting. The type of wood also informs the cutting method for the best results.

Good Woods for Carving

Wood is classified into softwood and hardwood. Softwood is easier to carve than hardwood, which makes it ideal for whittling. Several softwood options were explored in the previous book, including basswood, balsa, butternut, pine, and a few others. This section presents woods suitable for intermediate carvers. They are a bit more challenging to use, but none of these woods are too hard to carve. Both cherry and maple wood is grown commercially in the United States and Canada, so they are readily accessible. The latter two options, mahogany, and tupelo are available here but they are not grown commercially. However, some woods feature these trees and timber yards may source them on request.

Cherry

Cherry wood comes from the Latin species known as *Prunus serotina*. The wood is moderately difficult to work with but is an attractive option because of its color. Cherry wood has rich reddish brown hues that look stunning when a clear coat of finish is applied after carving. The wood becomes darker as it ages, even during the drying process.

Carving fine details into cherry wood is possible, so you can use it to produce beautifully textured designs. Cherry wood is a popular choice for wood crafts and construction, which increases the price greatly. If you do go with cherry wood for your project, then practice your cuts on a cheaper wood before you start your main design to avoid ruining an expensive cut. Additionally, do not use power tools with cherry wood as it burns the surface. However, it is perfectly suitable for woodworking done by hand.

Maple

Maple wood is another popular carver's choice but you need some patience to produce a masterpiece. There are two types of maple trees for carving, namely, the *Acer saccharum*, which is a hard variety, and the softer *Acer rubrum*, which is ideal for carvers. Maple is reasonably priced and readily available at timber yards.

Figure grain is prevalent in maple and can add an aesthetic quality to your finished product. Just remember that grain patterns create carving challenges so you have to work carefully while carving maple, as the grain density changes throughout any wood segment. Some of the grain patterns seen in maple are curly, bird's eye, tiger, and fiddleback. The grain texture forces carvers to work carefully so maple lends itself well to highly detailed carvings. Finish your maple artwork by polishing the wood to a glossy shine.

Mahogany

Mahogany, with the Latin name *Swietenia macrophylla*, grows in many countries across the world although the greatest number come from Central America. It is sometimes called Honduras mahogany. A medium to coarse texture makes it a bit more challenging to carve, although the grain is relatively straight with few interlocked areas.

Mahogany is a great choice if you plan on having a natural-looking project since the color plays beautifully through the wood. The hues range from light to dark and include reddish-brown and rich, deep reds. This interplay of colors looks great in relief carving, for boxes, and larger projects that display the colors. Mahogany is used frequently for making furniture or decorative panels.

Tupelo

Tupelo is a type of black gum tree but the name is confusing because the wood's color is light. Tupelo has interlocked grain with a uniform texture, which does not split easily. It is a challenging wood to work with, as the grain is tight and varied, but the final result is rewarding for any carver. The color of Tupelo ranges from light to pale brown and may have patches with a gray hue. It takes various colors well, so try staining Tupelo as a finish.

When selecting wood, choose a piece that is large enough for your design but not too big that there is a lot of excess stock. Consider the grain pattern, colors, and finished product before you choose your blank. Ensure the wood is suitable for your application and that there are no inherent issues that weaken your finished product. Although wood is your primary material, you can avoid damaging the wood by keeping your tools sharp.

Chapter 6:
Know the Sharpening Stones

A sharp blade is important for wood carving activities. Razor-sharp blades slide through wood easily and require less force to move across or against the grain. Unwanted directional changes and cutting yourself occur when a blade is dull. So, prioritize sharpening your bladed tools.

Secret Twelve: The right tools are important. But, using sharp tools is crucial. Improper tool care and not sharpening tools correctly using specific techniques with the right equipment causes problems. Replacing your tools becomes a frequent occurrence if your blades are dull and damaged due to incorrect or lack of maintenance. Additionally, your carving quality decreases as a dull knife causes damage.

Detailed care keeps your tools in the best condition possible. Sharpening blades requires two distinct steps. Firstly, shape a proper cutting angle using a sharpening stone. Secondly, polish the blade for a razor-sharp edge (Ellenwood, 2008, p. 201). Another term for this process is honing, which means to sharpen and refine a blade.

Various sharpening stones are available including oil, diamond, water, ceramic, and Arkansas stones. Ellenwood suggests the pros and cons of these stones, as shown under each type of stone below (2008, p. 202-219). Each one has specific characteristics, so find one that works for your blades.

Oil Stones

Among the most popular sharpening tools, the oil stone is probably the one you are most familiar with. Oil stones are cut from various materials. Novaculite, commonly known as an Arkansas stone, is discussed later in this chapter. Other options include Aluminium Oxide and Silicon Carbide.

Aluminum Oxide is a man-made stone and a popular option for sharpening. Besides fast cutting, Aluminium Oxide stones assist in refining the edge. Usually orange or brown in color, the stones have grits titled coarse, medium, and fine. Yet, these stones are coarser than Arkansas stones. Use Aluminium Oxide stones for sharpening and then move to Arkansas stones for further detailing.

Silicone Carbide is another popular option, as it cuts the fastest of all oil stones. Silicone Carbide stones come in coarse, medium, and fine grits, but do not create a fine edge. The coarse nature of these stones makes them best for initial shaping and sharpening. It has a gray color. Silicone Carbide stones are available readily and inexpensive.

Swarf removal, commonly known as metal filing, requires additional oil on the stone during sharpening. Using oil can be messy, so have a dedicated work area for sharpening with oil stones. Always clean blades thoroughly after using oil stones to remove any residue, otherwise the oil transfers to the wood causing stains.

Pros:

- Reasonable pricing

- Relatively fast cutting

- Combination stones are available

- Require little maintenance

Cons:

- Finer grits not available

- Cups with repeated usage

- Oil transfer to blades results in wood staining

Diamond Stones

Diamond stones consist of a metal plate topped with tiny diamonds. These diamonds are either mono-crystalline or poly-crystalline, although the former is longer lasting and more desirable. Industrial-grade diamonds make up the surface, which creates a harder stone. As a result, you apply less pressure while achieving faster sharpening. The diamonds increase the price of these stones and make them very expensive. However, they last much longer than other stones, which equalizes the costs in the long-run.

Diamond stones come in two styles. The first type has small holes, sharpens quickly, and catches swarf in the crevices. The second type has an uninterrupted diamond surface, which does not catch swarf and is ideal for sharpening pointed tools. Both types of diamond stones are available in various grits. Sometimes, an extra coarse diamond stone is utilized when flattening water or oil stones.

Pros:

- Fastest cutting stone

- Available in various grits

- Flatness remains ±0.002 of an inch

- Requires less pressure

- Lower maintenance than other stones

- Works with honing oil, water, or dry

- Unbreakable

Cons:

- Expensive

- Lighter pressure requires a mental adjustment

Water Stones

Water stones use water in the sharpening process. Although both synthetic and natural water stones exist, natural stones are not easy to come by. Synthetic stones dominate the market as they are available more readily. Regardless of the material, water stones are a bit more expensive than some of the other options.

Aluminum Oxide is the main component of synthetic water stones. It is the same material used in some oil stones but the adhesives combining the material differ. Water stones sharpen blades quickly as they are soft and reveal a new cutting surface often. As the blade moves across the stone, it removes surface material. However, the new sharper surface creates unevenness and requires flattening for continuous use.

Available in numerous grits, water stones are suitable for shaping and polishing blades. Soaking the stone in water before use is mandatory, but never let it freeze as it causes permanent damage. Additionally, dry your tools properly after sharpening to avoid rust formation.

Pros:

- Available in a variety of grits (coarse to extra fine)

- Fast cutting

- A single stone set can hone, shape, and sharpen

- Fine and extra-fine grits work well for polishing

Cons:

- Slightly more expensive

- Coarse grits erode rapidly

- Requires frequent flattening

- Requires water soaking

- Water may cause rust on tools

- Freezing wet stones are an issue

Ceramic Stones

Ceramic stones are constructed from a ceramic material, usually clay or other earthly compounds. The construction of ceramic stones produces a hard surface, which does not require any fluids for cutting. Yet, some people achieve better results when adding a touch of fluid. These stones are available as either a rod or a block and range in grit from medium to ultra-fine.

A variation of this stone is the ceramic water stone. An adhesive binds the individual ceramic materials together, which require water for proper cutting. However, you do not need to soak a ceramic water stone. Just add some water during the sharpening process. Ceramic water stones are available in numerous grits that do not wear as easily as other water stones. They are durable and do not erode quickly.

Pros:

- Superfine grits available

- Durable wear

- Low maintenance with infrequent flattening

Cons:

- Expensive

- Delicate and brittle

- Slow cutting

- Only available in fine grits

Arkansas Stones

Arkansas stones are a naturally occurring type of oil stone. Quarried in Arkansas, these stones are shaped and graded in the United States. Arkansas stones use a mineral oil during sharpening, although some people use them as water stones but that requires additional care. Pores in the stone may clog up with swarf, so never use the stone dry. They range from soft to hard, with each stone having unique characteristics.

Arkansas stones come in various colors, which often correspond with their grit type. Rather than using grit, Arkansas stones have hardness and density gradings. A coarse stone is soft and less dense, with Soft Arkansas ranging in grit from 600-800. Although some people use only a coarse stone, it does leave some bite to the edge. Finer Arkansas stones are hard and very dense, which makes them ideal for honing blades. The Hard Arkansas stone has a grit between 800 - 1000, while 1200+ associates with Hard Translucent or Hard Black Arkansas stones.

Pros:

- Simultaneous polishing and sharpening

- Mirror-like finish

- Slower erosion

- Works best for final blade honing

- Natural stone obtainable in four grades

Cons:

- Expensive

- Slow cutting

- Only fine grits available

Sharpening stones come in many materials, each with distinct qualities. No right or wrong stone exists, so, select the stones that work best for your tools. Sometimes, a combination of stones work best, so you can always grow your stone selection as you add new tools to your workshop.

Chapter 7:
Finish it the Right Way

Finishing your masterpiece with an oil or lacquer protects the wood from dust, grime, and decay. Additionally, it intensifies the wood grain by enhancing the different hues and textures. Two types of finishes are popular among woodcarvers: surface and penetrating finishes. While surface finishes are easy to apply, it remains on the surface of the wood only. However, a penetrating finish is more durable, as it infiltrates the wood grain.

Secret Thirteen*: Finishes add aesthetic quality and protect your pieces. Don't be afraid to play with several colors and textures, but, be careful of how you mix them. Putting one type of finish over another can destroy your hard work completely.*

Surface Finishes

Applying a surface finish protects the exterior of a piece and does not penetrate the wood. These finishes include varnish, shellac, and lacquer. Most have a natural appearance, although some finishes may darken the piece.

Surface finishes are easy to apply, which makes them a popular choice.

Varnish

Varnish is oil-based with additives including solvent and resin, which provides a transparent finish to the wood. The gloss option provides a shiny surface finish, while the satin and flat options dry to flatter colors through the addition of flattening agents. Always mix flat and satin varnish before application, as the agents settle to the base of the tin. Apply varnish over bare, stained, or painted wood. Although it can be used before a wax coating, the varnish will not adhere when applied over surface wax or in conjunction with other varnish brands (Ellenwood, 2008, p. 420). Although varnish dries slowly, it provides protection from UV light making it an ideal choice for many products.

Read the label on your chosen product for specific application instructions. Always clean your workspace before application otherwise dust is trapped within the varnish and creates a rough finish. A natural paintbrush, rag, or roller is suitable for varnish application. A warmer day is best for applying varnish, as cold and humid conditions slow the drying time. A very hot day is not ideal either since bubbles form on the surface when the varnish dries too quickly.

Apply a thin coat of varnish and leave it in a clean area for a 24-hour drying period. Apply a thicker second coat and additional coats, letting the piece dry fully between applications until you are satisfied with the finish. Most pieces require two to three coats, as varnish is a thicker finish. If your first coat has imperfections or rough patches, then use a very fine grit sandpaper.

Water-Based Varnish

Water-based varnish is a great choice if time is running out on your project, as it dries quickly and has very little odor. It is suitable for use over any dry surface or underneath wax. However, it does not do well on wet surfaces or when combined with other varnishes (Ellenwood, 2008, p. 422). Water-based finishes are thin and dry to a clear film with a natural feel, which lends it to many purposes. Most water-based varnishes do well on indoor items but it is not always suitable for items being used outdoors, as it is not heat-resistant.

Apply a water-based varnish with a rag or brush (preferably with natural bristles). Always stir your can of varnish, as shaking it creates bubbles that ruin the final product. Alternatively, purchase a spray varnish for faster application but shake it properly to mix the contents. Spray varnish creates a very thin layer over the wood, so it may require several coats for a proper finish. The thin consistency of water-based varnish may cause it to run down the wood if you apply a thick coat. Rather, take your time in applying four to five thin coats, leaving ample time for each coat to dry before the next application.

Shellac

Shellac is a wax-based finish sourced from bugs that live in trees. A variety of colors sets this surface varnish apart from others and dries to a glossy finish. Apply shellac over bare wood, varnish, alcohol-free stains, and paint. Shellac does not agree with alcohol, so never apply an alcohol-based finish over it. Additionally, do not apply shellac when the weather is humid or on damp wood (Ellenwood, 2008, p. 425). Shellac is quick-drying with an easy application process.

Shellac has sealing properties, making it an ideal choice for many projects. Scraped from trees, this bug secretion is flaky after processing but mixing it with alcohol creates the wax. Most shellac comes premixed, so you do not have to mix it all. However, you can purchase the flakes alone and make your wax mixture.

Apply shellac with a brush or pad it on with a thick rag. Shellac dries rapidly, so apply it liberally to prevent any missed spots. Some woodworkers apply shellac with a brush then run a rag over it immediately after application to remove any imperfections. Sand the piece with a fine-grit paper and remove any dust with a clean cloth before applying a second coat. Apply up to five coats for a glossy finish or sand it with super-fine paper to create a satin finish. Shellac may dry to a white film but this is rubbed off with a soft, clean cloth.

Lacquer

Lacquer is a solvent-based option and very thin, which enables rapid drying. After application by spraying, it penetrates the wood more than other surface finishes and enhances the wood's natural grain. Apply lacquer over bare wood, water-based stains, or shellac. Seal the wood with lacquer before applying stain or wax, but never use it with oil-based stains or varnish (Ellenwood, 2008, p. 428). Most lacquers contain tree resin, although modern variants combine it with nitrocellulose, which is another type of resin.

Lacquer application is done by either a brush or spray. If you decide to use a brush, then purchase a natural-bristle brush and apply a thin coat. Do not brush over the same area repeatedly, as the lacquer becomes sticky. Rather, work quickly, let the lacquer dry, and then add additional coats. Lacquer sprays come in aerosol bottles or as a liquid for spray guns. Whichever one you choose, apply a thin, even coat and allow to dry before adding more coats. Spray-based lacquers contain solvents with strong odors, so only apply them in well-ventilated areas and away from fire.

Paste Wax

Paste wax is an older option but remains popular among woodcarvers. Although it requires extra elbow grease, the application is easy and the costs are low. Paste wax works over any finish or bare wood, but do not use it as a bottom coat under varnish. Although the wax is solid initially, dissolve it in a mineral-spirit solvent or toluene to make a paste for application (Ellenwood, 2008, p. 430). Paste wax is made from beeswax, paraffin, Carnauba wax, or other agents.

Wax comes in many colors, so you have a range of options to finish your piece. Select a wax that has a similar color to your wood. This matching produces the best possible result, as using darker or lighter wax may not look as great. Use a clean cloth to apply the wax in a motion similar to polishing your shoes. Wax does not dry completely, so leave a minimum of 24 hours between applications. Most pieces only need one or two coats. Sanding between coats is not recommended because the wax remains damp.

Stain

Wood stain is another surface finish but penetrates the wood and changes the color. The purpose of stain is to darken the wood's color so that it makes the grain more visible. However, it does not protect the wood and requires additional surface finishing for wood nourishment and protection. Apply stain to bare or sanded wood but do not use it as a top coat, as it provides no protection for the wood.

A stain is a great option when your current piece does not match other furniture and trims in your home. When applied over lighter woods, stains provide a rich tone and change the color; that is why many stain colors receive their names from other trees. Apply wood stain with a brush or clean muslin cloth. Work quickly to avoid dripping and leave the stain to absorb into the wood for several hours. Afterward, wipe down the entire piece using a clean cloth to remove any unabsorbed stain, then let the piece dry.

Penetrating Finishes

Penetrating oils are a favored option by woodcarvers as it has many advantages. Besides giving a natural finish, penetrating oils enhance the grain, do not cause build-up, and provide a low luster shine, which looks similar to satin. A major benefit of penetrating oils is that the finish does not peel or crack, making it a kitchen and child-friendly choice.

All wood contains natural oils but these oils dry out over time. Finishing your wood with a natural oil replaces the wood's original oil and provides nourishment. Once applied, the oil penetrates the wood grain and settles into the capillaries. Afterward, the oil hardens (called self-polymerization) through an oxidation process. Yet, it does not become as hard as surface finishes.

Wood pieces that are handled infrequently work well with penetrating oils. Think about picture frames, wood trims, sculptures, and display cabinets. These items are not used daily, so a penetrating oil is great to keep them in pristine condition. However, most penetrating oils are free from or low in volatile organic compounds (VOC), so they are used for kitchen utensils, cutting boards, and wooden toys that sometimes travel to a child's mouth.

Penetrating oils come in three types: pure, polymerized, and hardwax.

- Pure oils are 100% natural, food-safe, and dry slowly. Apply the oil to bare wood and leave it for about 15 minutes, then wipe off any residue. Repeat this process five to eight times. It can take several weeks for the piece to dry properly, so do not rush the process.

- Polymerized oils dry faster, are food-safe, and shinier. Manufacturers complete the polymerization process by heating the oil without any oxygen. Apply polymerized (sometimes called boiled) oil onto bare wood and wait at least 15 minutes, then remove any residue from the piece. You can apply additional coats but it is not necessary. Give your work a couple of days for drying.

- Hardwax oils are a blend of vegetable oils and other components, such as beeswax. It creates a wax-like finish, has water-resistance, and dries quite quickly. However, a damp piece is not food-safe. Only use the finished piece for food preparation purposes once it dries completely.

Linseed Oil

Linseed oil is the first choice of many woodcarvers. It gives a classic, plain appearance to the wood while maintaining the original color. It prevents unnecessary cracks by strengthening the interior and exterior of the piece.

There are pure and boiled linseed options. The boiled variety dries much faster, usually within 18 hours. It is water-repellant and stops chalking, which makes it a great choice for finishing antiques and furniture. The drying agents can be abrasive, so use gloves during application.

Danish Oil

Danish oil is a suitable option for products stored indoors. This oil permeates wood deeply and works well on tight grains. It might include a varnish agent to promote shine. Some Danish oils have a walnut color, which adds warmth to the wood but does change the color slightly. Successive applications are required but may darken the color more, so some use it for initial applications and then use other oils for later coats. Most Danish oils are polymerized varieties, so always check the labels if you seek pure oil.

Teak Oil

Teak oil is a possibility for challenging woods, such as teak, mahogany, and rosewood. Deep penetration of the oil nourishes the wood without leaving a film on the surface. It is a quick-drying oil with properties that make it UV and water-resistant. These qualities make teak oil ideal for use around water features and maritime purposes but do not submerge the wood. Some teak oils darken the wood slightly and are unsuitable for softer woods. Teak oil works best when applying it with a cloth, although some people use a brush.

Tung Oil

Tung oil is suitable for use on its own or as a complementary product for other finishes. It is a clear oil with less gloss than other varieties, which provides a classic finish. Wood or carving imperfections are hidden when applying teak oil, as the satin finish lessens their appearance. Teak oil resists mildew and water, which makes it a versatile product. These qualities of teak oil often make it a great choice for the reconditioning of finished items.

Mineral Oil

Mineral oil differs slightly from other oils. It does not oxidize and cannot dry, as it is a petroleum distillate. Mineral oil repels moisture, is non-toxic, and does not change the color of the wood. It is suitable for use on toys and kitchen utensils. However, mineral oil continuously requires reapplication as it washes and rubs off easily. Some people use mineral oil with wax to make it last longer.

Walnut Oil

Another carver's favorite is walnut oil. Most walnut oils are non-toxic and safe for use on food items, so use it on utensils or butcher blocks. Walnut oil does not darken the wood but rather restores natural grain. It lasts longer than mineral oil and dries faster, as additional ingredients speed up oxidation. The finished product has a satin-feel and works best in warmer conditions.

A word of caution. Generally, most finishes are food-safe but that does not mean all of them are suitable. Always read the label on your specific product to check what it can be used for. Quick-drying products usually contain agents that make them unsuitable for use in food preparation or children's toys. Double-check the instructions and cautions on your products, especially if you have not used them in some time.

All wood pieces require care to maintain it in pristine condition. Whether it is a butcher block, toys, a rocking chair, or kitchen utensils, they require some attention once in a while. Goods handled frequently need more conditioning, but you should be able to tell when it is necessary. Recondition any item that appears dry by applying a generous amount of oil. Choose the best option for your masterpiece and apply a suitable finishing product. Leave it to dry and then display it in all its glory!

Chapter 8:
Get to Work

It is time to put your new skills to the test! You have all the knowledge you need to attempt a myriad of projects. Try your hand at the following projects that use whittling basics and the wood carving techniques shown in the first two chapters. Be patient while carving because you are still learning the skills. Do not take the process too seriously; rather, focus on making the cuts correctly and practice with several tools.

Secret Fourteen: *Plan ahead before you start carving. Sketch out your design and do some research. Always use a cheaper piece of wood to practice cuts that you will make later on in the project rather than ruining your masterpiece.*

Happy Mouse

Figurines, comic book characters, and animal silhouettes are great templates for incised carving. For this design, a happy mouse is at the center of the creation but instead of just a silhouette, additional details like a face and clothing are added. Practice the design on a cheap piece of softwood before carving it into a hardier wood, or keep it on softwood like balsa for painting later on. Start with a smooth piece of wood measuring 4" x 4" x ⅓".

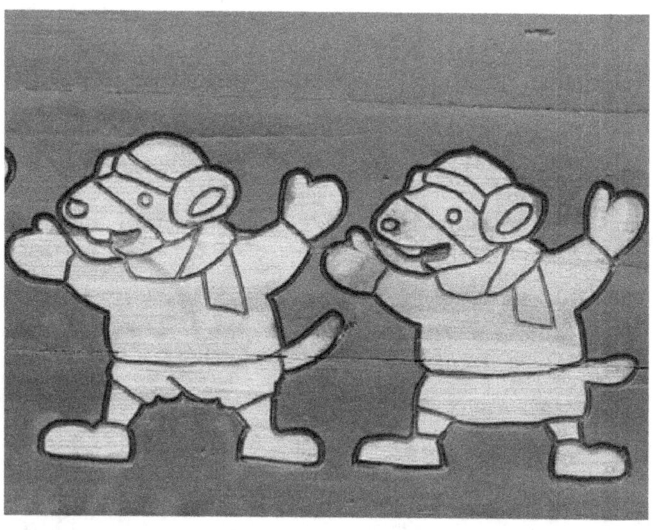

Instructions

1. Find a picture of a mouse, or use the one shown, as a template and transfer it to the wood.

2. Use a detail knife to make an initial cut around the exterior outline then carve the outline deeper with a veiner.

3. Carve the interior details like the scarf, shirt, and boots with a detail knife then use precision cuts to carve the facial features.

4. Go over any lines that you want to define more and check that the outline is slightly thicker than the interior detail lines.

5. Finish the mouse in any way you want. The one shown has a painted background, dark stain in the incised lines, and a natural finish to the main image.

Coaster Set

Drink coasters are ideal for practicing your new wood carving techniques, especially incise carving. You can use any type of wood and harder options work too because of the greater control in carving finer details. Additionally, coasters require less wood for carving providing a cost-effective first introduction to intermediate wood types like mahogany. The instructions for this set of coasters use square blanks, but you can also make round or polygon-shaped blanks. The sky's the limit with coasters so dream big! Most coaster sets contain four or six in a pack but you can carve more or less. The design for this set is not set in stone; you can use any line pattern you want! Start by getting together six pieces of wood measuring 3 ½" x 3 ½" x ¼".

__Secret Fifteen__: Don't be afraid to sketch your own designs. While there is nothing wrong with copying patterns and projects, drawing your own ideas can make you a better carver. You will start thinking more about proportions and dimensions, and boost your creativity.

Instructions

1. Use a pencil to draw a ¼" border on the inside of each blank. Make a second border by drawing the lines a ⅛" from the inside of the first border. Draw a third border a ⅛" from the previous one. You should have three borders in total.

2. Draw any design in the middle of each coaster. You can use the same design on all six or use a theme to create a different design on each coaster. For example, you may want a geometric theme, so draw a five-pointed star on

one coaster, a double-pointed arrow on the next coaster, and so forth. Another theme could be fish and might include sharks, pufferfish, and bass.

3. Use a thin veiner to score the second border. Use long strokes and a low grip to carve a straight line. Next, use a detail knife and cut into the first and third borders. These borders should be thinner than the one in the middle, which creates a contrasting pattern.

4. Cut out the central design on each coaster using a detail knife or veiner. The choice is up to you, so decide whether you want a thin or thick incise carving. Play with several options until you find something you like. Just remember that you can widen the cut from a detail knife by running it over again or using a veiner but you cannot add wood once you make a wider cut.

5. Check that your incised carving has equal depths across all cuts by using a gauge such as a toothpick or a thin metal plate.

6. At this stage, the incised carving of the design is finished. You can add extra details to your design as you see fit. One idea is to change the square corners into round ones by using a microplane or rasp to remove the angled corner.

7. Sand the coasters and remove any stray wood slivers. Add a finish of your choice: paint the incised cuts, add a contrasting stain, or leave it as is. Finish the coasters with a protective, water-resistant coating as you will be placing glasses with liquid on it. You may want to apply a maintenance finishing coat every few months for durability.

Bottle Holder

Most people have at least one bottle of wine in the house and this bottle holder is ideal for holding your wine. Alternatively, use it to hold your bottle of olive oil or balsamic vinegar. This bottle holder has an intricate chip carving design, which looks difficult but is quite easy to carve thanks to the repetitive pattern. Use a piece of butternut or balsa measuring 12" x 3 ½" x 1", as it is easier to carve. Below is the pattern for the holder. You will need a detail knife and chip cutting knife with a thin point for this project.

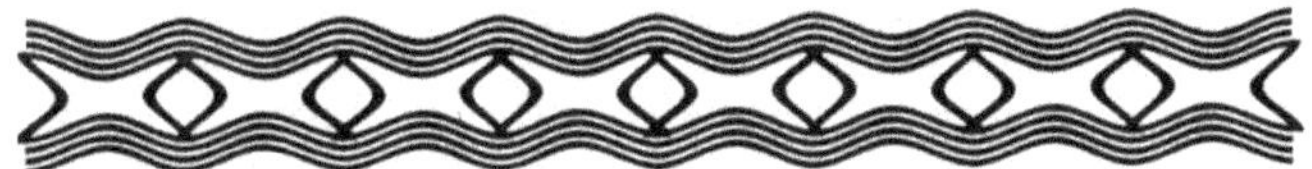

Instructions

1. Cut an angle into one of the small sides to form the base of the holder. The base should be cut at an angle of 37 degrees.

2. Cut a circle at the top of the holder (opposite the cut base) for the bottle's neck to fit into. The hold should have a diameter of 1 ⅜" and be located about 1" from the smaller top side. You can either carve the hole by hand using gouges or do it faster by drilling a hole with a power tool.

3. Draw a rectangular border that is ⅛" wide on all the sides of the block. Use a detail knife to create a very shallow scoring cut all around. Also make a ⅛" border around the circle on both sides.

4. Transfer the pattern to the lengthwise edge of the larger flat face that will be the front. Transfer it all along the block

by moving the pattern to fit snuggly below the previous one; you want the curves to lie inside each other. Hold the wood with a quick-change clip as you transfer the pattern to the wood. It frees up both hands for working and secures the pattern to ensure it does not move and skew the design.

5. This pattern will be chip-carved using a series of cuts, as explained in the relevant chapter. Make a stop cut along each long wave using a detail knife. Try to do it on the right of each line, then use a chip knife to do free-form chip cutting along the wavy lines. Take your time in making each cut, as the angles change. However, the softer wood and a thin cut make it possible to remove the chip in a single glide. Repeat this process with every wavy line.

6. Next, we will start the second series of cuts, which will remove the diamond shapes between the waves but first, you have to create stop cuts. Make a straight wall cut along one side of each diamond. Remember that series cutting requires you to cut the same side of each diamond in the pattern before starting

on the next side. Once you are done with
one side of the diamond, move to the
third and fourth sides. These straight-
wall cuts will be used later in the design.

7. Move onto the actual diamond removal
    by using the four-sided hand position.
    Keep a very small area (ridge) between
    the previously made straight cut and the
    diamond chip. Once again, work
    through the diamond in a series method,
    rather than removing the entire chip in
    one go.

8. Now remove the hour-glass shaped
    wood between the diamonds and the
    waves by using the sloped plane to
    straight-wall method. Keep using the
    series method for consistency. The
    entire front should be carved at this
    point in time.

9. Repeat steps four to nine on the back
    panel of the bottle holder. If you are up
    for a challenge, you can chip carve the
    pattern into the sides as well for extra
    detail. In this case, you will place the
    pattern in the middle of the facing side
    rather than repeating it several times.

10. Tap the wood lightly against your hand to remove any stray chips. Use rifflers and needle files to smooth out the cuts then go over them with fine sandpaper. Apply a satin-finish lacquer for protection. You can use a paintbrush to apply a darker stain into the wave areas for extra accentuation.

Decorative Box

Chip carving is a staple technique on all types of boxes such as jewelry boxes or storage containers. Many elaborate designs can be carved into boxes. Some designs have only a few details, while others consist of many triangles, circles, and other shapes creating a complex design. For this project, you need a wooden box to carve into and the panels should be at least a ¼" thick. You can build your own box too but a pre-assembled box is suitable. Choose a box made from softwood so that you can carve the design easily. A bar or pipe clamp can be useful for holding the box while you are busy carving. However, rubber bands or web clamps work well to secure the box to a workbench.

Instructions

1. Find a piece of paper that is the same size as the top of the box to draw a design on. This design will be transferred to the top of the box once you are ready to start carving. It is not advisable to draw intricate patterns directly onto the wood, as it is difficult to correct lines drawn in mistake.

2. Design a pattern for the top of the box. It can be anything you want but try to include both a fine triangle and free-form carving elements. For example, you could draw a circular, mandala type design in the middle of the lower half of the box with curves and spirals around it. Alternatively, draw a decorative series pattern across the diagonal and add leaves around the sides of the diagonal stripe. Transfer the pattern to the top of the box.

3. Start carving the design by making straight wall cuts where necessary and score any lines where chips will be removed.

4. Use a chip knife and the three or four-sided method to remove geometric objects. Always work in a series form by cutting into one side of the shape throughout the entire pattern and then moving onto the next side.

5. Next, make free-form cuts for any swirls and curved elements in your design. Try to tap a chisel or gouge with a mallet for extra cutting practice with different tools. Keep your angles at relevant levels and do not apply to much force.

6. Check the depth of your cuts with a gauge and correct those that are not deep enough. Keep in mind that chip carving preferably requires a single cut into each line, as subsequent cuts may remove too much wood and spoil your design.

7. The carving on the top of the box is complete. You can leave it as is, or add decorative elements to the sides of the box, according to your preferences.

8. Use needle files and rifflers to clean up the inside of each cut pattern and line.

Aim to get into all the tight corners for a perfect finish.

9. Finish the box by adding a stain with a coat of wax or oil.

Wall Sign

Sign making uses many carving techniques. The alphabet project in Chapter 2 used relief carving but some signs have the text going into the wood, which requires intaglio techniques. Remember that chip carving forms part of intaglio, so most intaglio projects have elements of chip carving at some stage. Choose any word of your liking for this project. I have chosen the word "Friends" for my sign, although "welcome" and "love" are popular options too. This is the ideal opportunity to use a harder wood, such as cherry or mahogany, and you need a piece cut to 12" x 4" x ½". If this design seems too small, then use a larger font and tools that suit you better.

Instructions

- Select your wood and change it to a font with some more details. A serif font that has little corners is a great choice to practice fine carving details. Print the pattern and transfer it to the wood.

- Draw a ½" border and a second border ⅛" from the first on the front of the panel to create a frame for your design. Use a v-gouge to cut a square trough by making long shallow strokes. First, place the tool at an almost perpendicular angle to the left side and make a cut. Second, change the angle so that the blade is at an almost perpendicular angle to the right side. Finally, finish the square trough by cutting down the middle of the trough to define the angle of the cut border.

- You need both hands to carve this piece, so secure your blank wood to the workbench using a clamping device of your choice. C-clamps are a great option but you can use other clamps too.

- Use a ¼" inch v-gouge with a 60-degree angle to carve the letters. Make single pass troughs along the lengths of the straight letters using a low grip. Cutting curves like in the "e" are slightly more challenging, so you might want to swap out the v-gouge for a rounded gouge that fits onto your letter and carve it at the relevant angles using the free-form chip carving technique. After making the first trough, insert a toothpick and mark it for a depth gauge to use in subsequent cuts.

- Add the serif details to each letter by placing a thin gouge at an angle to the wood and tap it lightly with a small mallet towards the inside of the letter. Cut the dot for the "i" using the globe cut method.

- Remove any wood slivers with rasps while focusing on getting into all the tight corners. For an extra feature, incise

or chip carve a patterned border. Sand
the rest of the wood and apply any finish
you want.

Flower Panel

If you want to practice intaglio carving,
then this project is ideal for you. It is a wood
panel artwork that contains a variety of flowers
to practice carving at different depths using a
range of fundamental cuts. Select a softwood
for this design or opt for tupelo or another
light-colored wood as this piece is one that
does well with paint. You do not have to use
expensive wood, since most of the flowers no
longer have the natural wood showing after
painting. This wood panel is suitable for
hanging as artwork, so choose a reasonably
sized piece of wood, measuring about 15" x 10"
x ¾". This panel is a larger size than you may
be used to working with and the intaglio
carving technique could push the panel along
the workbench. Hold the panel to your
workbench with suitable size clamps.

Instructions

1. Print flower templates from the internet
    that have a clear outline and some
    internal features. Choose five flowers to

use, such as a daisy, jasmine flower, hibiscus, cosmos, and plumeria. You want to create a pattern that has flowers facing towards you, with separate petals and not too much detail. Transfer the flower patterns to the top half of the panel and alternate their heights for a bit of playfulness. Draw a stem and leaves onto the bottom half and add a few clumps of grass at the very bottom of the panel.

2. Remember the basics of intaglio is to carve into the wood and the items closest to your view in real life will be the deepest cuts. Start by carving the grass. Score each blade of grass on the outside and add a thin line to the middle. Next, make a very shallow cup cut from the middle to the one side of each blade of grass and a deeper cup cut towards the other side. The sides of the grass should be deeper than the middle as they are closer in an actual view. You can use different cutting depths for the grass as some blades are closer to the viewer than others.

3. Carve the first flower, which is a daisy according to this pattern, although you

can use any flower since the steps remain similar. The anther is closest to the viewer and will be the deepest, while the petals have shallower cuts. Score a globe around the anther (inside circle) of the flower to create a stop cut, then use a medium gouge to make a globe cut. Next, work on alternating petals and carve them using a single pass ellipse cut. Carve the remaining alternating petals in the same way but make your pass shallower than the previous one to create the illusion of depth. Carve the stem of the daisy by making a single pass through from between the grass and into the petals. The stem should be shallow. Carve any leaves using the same process as the grass blades, by making cup cuts. Use a veiner to add detail to the anther by making tiny dimples into the globe.

4. The next flower is a jasmine flower, which has distinct petals with a clear separation between them. Use a jasmine pattern that has five wider petals. Mark the anther first by making a small scoring circle and remove only a small bit of wood from it as the anther is the part that is the furthest away from the

viewer. Next, carve each petal separately but note the changes in depth. The tips of the petals are closest to the viewer so they will be the deepest carved area. Initially, carve each petal by using the multiple pass ellipse technique, then use your detail knife to carve the tips of the petals deeper and taper them towards the anther. Carve the leaves and stem in the same way as you did with the daisy.

5. An open, front-facing hibiscus flower will have the pistil closest to you while the petals open towards the back and are the farthest away. However, the petals have a rounded shape with the inside of the petal being just as far back as the tips of the petal. Carve the petals first by making multiple pass ellipses for each petal. The petal must have a concave shape and be deeper along the middle. Work with one petal at a time and look carefully at your template to see the overlapping petal. The overlapping side should be carved at a shallower angle than the other petal. Next, create the pistil by using a veining tool to cut a single pass through from the middle of the flower and curve it towards one side. Run the veiner over the line again from

the middle to the tip to add depth, and
then make another pass right at the tip
to create the deepest area. Use the
veining tool to add the stamen segments
to the pistil. The stamen should be just
as deep, or deeper, than the pistil. Carve
the leaves and stem into the design.

6. Carve the cosmos flower by using a
   combination of the previous techniques.
   Make the anther using the globe cut
   shown for the daisy, then carve the
   petals using the instructions for jasmine.
   Pay attention to depth in the flower so
   that small details become present. Use a
   detail knife to add texture to each petal
   by cutting very shallow ridges from the
   anther to the tip of the petal.

7. The final flower is the plumeria, which
   has overlapping petals similar to the
   hibiscus. However, the plumeria's petals
   are narrower than the hibiscus and there
   is no clear anther. Score the petal lines
   where they meet on the inside of the
   flower as a guide, then carve each petal
   using the multiple pass ellipse method.
   Focus on depth and the overlapping
   petals to create dimension.

8. Once you are happy with your intaglio flower carving, use rifflers to remove any stray wood and to smooth out your design. Paint each flower in its traditional colors using acrylic paint and allow the paint to dry completely. Apply a spray lacquer over the entire panel and leave it to dry for several days. The panel is ready to be mounted on your wall or presented to someone as a handmade gift.

Scallop Shell Paperweight

Carving shells enables you to practice relief carving techniques and round moldings. There are many images of shells to work from or keep a shell on your workbench for inspiration. This pattern is taken from a design by Cindy Joslyn (2017). A softwood like butternut is a great option, although you may want to use cherry wood as it has the same color interplay as shells. Start with a block measuring 3" x 3" x 1 ½", as this is a deep relief piece. Wood in itself is not heavy enough to act as a paperweight, so a metal USS ⅞" flat washer adds the necessary weight and a felt covering avoids the bottom of the paperweight from scratching your desk surface.

Instructions

1. Use a compass to make a 3" circle inside
    both squares then use a gouge to remove
    excess wood around the circle so that
    you are left with a blank. A #3 gouge
    with a width of ⅞" works well to remove
    the excess wood stock without requiring
    a mallet. Alternatively, purchase a round
    blank measuring 3" in diameter to skip
    this step.

2. Measure ¾" from the bottom along the
    side of the blank and mark it all-around
    to indicate the relief line. Draw a scallop
    shell onto one face of the blank. Center
    it in the middle. You can use a template
    or do a freehand drawing.

3. Use a detail knife to make a stop cut
    around the shell's edge. Use the same
    gouge as previously to carve away the
    wood around the shell until it is level
    with the cutting line. You will have to
    deepen the stop cut as you carve away
    the excess wood. Use a flat gouge or
    chisel to create a level ledge around the
    shell.

4. Draw the shell's feature lines onto the wood and add an extension of these lines around the shell as reference points. These lines in the shell are called rays.

5. Create a stop cut with a detail knife between the teardrop shell and the triangular wings. Now, use the leveling technique to carve the wings until they are only an ⅛" high.

6. Round out the shell shape with a pocket knife until it is the desired shape on all sides.

7. Make a stop cut along each shell cap, which is the horizontal line over the shell using a detail knife, then make a gouge cut along these lines to emphasize the cut. The shell usually has three cap lines.

8. Define the smallest ray section by making v-cuts along each using a detail knife. Next, work on the other ray sections until all have a v-cut running through the ray. Detail the curvature between the rays by making gouge cuts.

9. Use a veiner to emphasize the wings by adding three lines into each.

10. Turn the paperweight around and trace the washer's external circle onto the wood. Make a ⅛ deep stop cut all along the circle then use the gouge to remove the wood inside the circle. The stop cut is a guide for depth but placing the washer into the recess will indicate if it is deep enough. The washer should lie flush (flat) with the wood and not protrude from it.

11. Glue the washer into the base then glue the felt piece to the bottom of the paperweight. Allow the glue to dry properly.

12. Finish the shell by applying linseed or danish oil with a paintbrush and check that you get it into all the thin cuts. Wipe any excess oil off the wood after an hour and let it dry overnight. You may want to add a second oil coat and then allow the piece to dry out over several days.

Bird on a Branch

Many relief carvings feature landscapes or scenes from nature. This design is no different, as it takes its inspiration from nature, and specifically, our beloved trees that produce wood. This project is a high relief carving of a bird sitting on a branch. It contains a variety of textures and methods, such as rounding and leveling. A lighter wood works best for this project, as it is painted afterward but you can use any type of wood if you want to retain the natural color. You need a block of wood measuring 10" x 6" x 1 ½" and this project includes chisel work, so keep those ready. C-clamps can secure the wood to your workbench while carving.

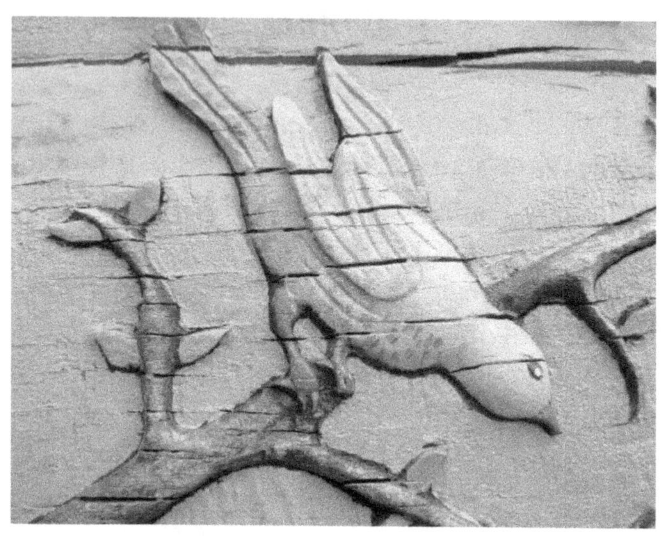

Instructions

1. Make a mark ⅔" from the top of each thinner side of the block and draw a line all around to designate the cutting level. Your relief carving will cut down this amount of wood from the top surface to reveal the design.

2. Transfer a pattern of a bird sitting on a branch to your wood. Extend the branches to reach the side of the block if necessary.

3. Make stop cuts all around the exterior outline of the design. The stop cuts can be relatively deep but do not force your

chisel into the wood with excessive force. A light tap will suffice. Use a #3 ⅞" gouge to remove the wood around the design. Deepen the stop cuts when necessary and continue shaving off wood from the background until it is at the ⅔" markings along the side of the board. Do not worry too much about creating a super flat plane, as ridging adds a textural element to the background.

4. Work on the leaves next to create the levels of the piece. Start by making a stop cut between the branch and each leaf. The leaves are thinner than the branch, so remove some of the surface on each leaf until it is ⅛" to ⅜" thick. The leaves can vary in height and have some slope to keep them looking real.

5. Use a detail knife to make stop cuts around the bird everywhere it touches the branch. Shape the branch by using gouge cuts to create roundness. The edges of the branch should be thinner than the middle section, so use a rounded tapering effect. Make any twigs or narrower branch sections thinner than the main branch but keep them

thicker than the leaves. Add a slight v-cut into areas where the branches and twigs meet for added detail.

6. Mold the basic shape of the bird by making gouge cuts. Add stop cuts where the beak, feet, and wings meet the body, then continue carving the rounded body from this point. Keep the back wing thinner and remove extra wood from the head, neck, and tail to shape the bird properly. Once you are happy with the main body, shape the wings. Add v-cuts on each wing to denote separate feathers.

7. Use a detail knife to cut the beak and feet, paying special attention to the toes and beak line. Make a light dimple cut for the eye. Use a detail knife with a very thin point and undercut the feet, as well as the twigs. These small details provide an extra dimension to the scene and set it apart from a simple carving.

8. Once all the shaping is done, use needle files to smooth out the carving and rifflers to get into the tight corners like the branch connections. Sand the

background to smooth it out to your liking.

9. Paint the entire scene in colors of your choice. Although the scene above is fully painted, I sometimes leave the branch and twigs the original wood color for a special touch. Once the paint dries, add a sealing layer and let it dry out over several days.

Portrait with a Border

Why not try your hand at a project that uses several of your new techniques together? The Portrait with a Border project is a facial portrait made using relief, incised, and chip carving, which is surrounded by a gouged border. Natural colors work best for this project, so use a wood that has some color variation. Cherry or mahogany is a popular option since they have rich hues in the wood. These wood choices are slightly harder and more challenging to work with but this project is perfect for honing your skills with new techniques on more expensive wood. As always, practice your cuts, or the entire project, on a cheaper piece of wood before starting the final project. The raw block should measure 12" x 9" x 1 ½". A thicker wood block is fine too but it cannot be thinner, as you will be cutting into the top ¾" of the block.

Instructions

1. On the flat, top carving surface draw a horizontal and vertical line through the middle of the block. You should now have four rectangles. Using these rectangles as a guide, draw a large ellipse onto the block. The ellipse should touch all four sides and be slightly further away from the corners.

2. Draw another ellipse towards the inside of the first, ensuring that a distance of 1" is kept between the two ellipses. These ellipses form the border of the portrait, which will look like a picture frame once done. Draw similar ellipses on the bottom surface of the block.

3. Use a ⅞" wide #3 gouge to remove the wood around the ellipse so that you are left with an elliptical blank. Try to make the cut sides as flat as possible for maximum effect. Secure the elliptical blank to your workbench by using clamps of your choice. This project is an odd size and you may need to place the

clamp directly onto the design, so keep a block of softwood between the work surface and the clamp.

4. Find a side-view portrait on the internet to use as inspiration for this project. Think about how coins often feature a side profile of an influential person's face - that is what you are aiming for. This project delivers a result similar to a coin. Transfer the pattern to the ellipse ensuring that the bottom of the pattern touches onto the inner ellipse but do not draw onto the frame. An older portrait where the person wears a hat or bonnet is a great choice.

5. Make a straight wall cut along the inner elliptical border and around the face's outline. Next, remove the background between the facial outline and the frame for the relief pattern. The background should have a depth of ¾" so use a ruler or gauge to check for consistency at various places.

6. Make a v-cut trough along the inner ellipse to define the picture frame. Use a ¼" #5 u-gouge to cut from the outer ellipse to the inside one all around the

frame to create a ridged pattern. Make the cut by using the double pass trough method but angle the blade as necessary along the roundings.

7. Shape the facial portrait next. First, make straight wall cuts using a detail knife everywhere you have a line, such as around the eyes, mouth, hairline, collar, etc. Second, work on defining the face by making gouge cuts to round the head, nose, mouth, and hair. Next, focus on the finer details and carve the eyes and mouth. Finally, use free-form chip carving to detail the hair. Continue carving until you are satisfied with the scene.

8. Use a second cut file to make a rounded edge along the outside of the frame. Use the cross filing method to smooth it out from the top and remove the harsh edge. Then round the frame along the inner ellipse using a second cut needle file. Smooth out any ridges and slivers in the portrait by using needle files and rifflers until the entire carving is void of roughness.

9. Use sandpaper of various grits to finish the outside of the block and parts of the frame and background.

10. Apply a thick layer of paste wax with a clean cloth over the entire piece. Focus on getting it into all the ridges and small areas. It may take some extra time and elbow grease but the finished product is well worth it.

Birdhouse

Every woodcarver wants to make a birdhouse at some time during their carving career. A birdhouse is a great project because you can practice a range of carving techniques. This specific design uses incised free-form chip carving and relief carving. Choose to build the birdhouse yourself or purchase a kit that contains all the pieces for easy assembly. Alternatively, purchase a pre-assembled birdhouse.

Requirements

The birdhouse requires four wall panels, a bottom, and a roof. Here are the relevant sizes for each:

- Roof: 7" x 6 ⅞" x ¾"

- Front panel: 7 ⅞" x 5" x ¾"

- Back panel: 8 ⅞" x 5" x ¾"

- Sides x2: 8 ⅞" x 5 ½" x ¾"

- Bottom: 5" x 4" x ¾"

The sides of the birdhouse must be cut at a 15-degree angle from the back to create a forward slant. The roof then rests on the slanted slope for water to run off it in case it gets wet.

Additional items are required to assemble the birdhouse, including dowels, supporting wood, and hinges. Since assembly is beyond the scope of this book, instructions are not given but can be found by doing a quick internet search. You will also need acrylic paint in a color of your choice and another finishing product such as lacquer or varnish.

Instructions

1. Prepare one side of the front, back, side, and bottom panels by applying a coat of acrylic paint. Let the paint dry thoroughly before moving to the next step. Do not add paint to the roof.

2. Start by drawing a design on the front panel. A nice design is a bird perched on a twig with a thicker branch in the background. Add some leaves to the twig for extra details. Use a veiner or #10 gouge to carve the outline of the bird, then add some feathers using the free-form cutting technique. You do not have to make very deep cuts for the design to show through the paint; just ensure you cut through the paint. Use a thin, medium depth gouge to carve the twig. Carve the thicker branch in the background by making incised cuts with a detail knife and add some extra short lines for bark texture.

3. Work on one side panel at a time. Draw a design that consists of a thick twig with thinner twigs extending from it. Add two or three leaves and some berries to the end of each twig. Use a 45-degree v-tool to carve the main twig from the bottom of the panel and curve it towards the top. You can apply lighter pressure to make the v-cut narrower towards the front, or use a thinner v-tool as you move along the cut. Use a veiner to carve the thinner twigs and leaves. You can change to a #9 or #10 gouge for

thicker leaves. Carve the berries by twirling the veiner around its axis. Repeat the process on the other panel but the designs do not have to be an exact match at all.

4. The bottom panel is not carved so move on to the roof for which you will relief carve shingles. Draw horizontal lines ¾" apart across the width of the roof. Next, draw vertical lines between the horizontal lines to create the shingles. Alternate the line spacing so that the shingles fit together like bricks rather than in straight lines. Using a v-gouge and the low grip carve stop lines through the horizontal grid, then turn the piece to carve each vertical line. Use a wide, flat gouge to accentuate each shingle by carving away excess wood so that individual shingles emerge. Define the horizontal lines with a detail knife in the middle of each. Use a triangular needle file to sand away any wood slivers.

5. Assemble the birdhouse walls and bottom. Check if your carving needs some additional twigs where the wood joins and add those with a veiner or gouge. Add the roof to the house then

apply a finishing like lacquer or varnish. A spray-type is easier to apply to a birdhouse but check that the finish you are using is water-resistant and offers UV protection. Let the piece dry and hang it in a suitable area to house birds.

Conclusion

I hope you are as excited as I am about wood carving! It truly is an amazing hobby with so many options for great projects. Basic whittling is a technique where you lose all track of time, as you carve out a handheld design. Now that you have mastered whittling, you are more than ready to move onto the intermediate projects in this book.

The first two chapters introduced four new techniques suitable for intermediate whittlers. These carving techniques are based on whittling and use similar tools. Incised and chip carving are fundamental to many wood carving designs, while intaglio and relief carving brings elaborate designs to life. Interestingly, all four techniques are connected in some way or another. Incised carving is the first step in most carving projects, while chip carving is a subset of intaglio. Relief carving is the opposite of intaglio as the carving protrudes rather than lying into the wood.

The different hand positions and grips assist in manipulating tools used for carving. Although the intermediate techniques use whittling knives, there are additional tools necessary for carving properly. Increase your tool collection with gouges, knives, chisels, and mallets for specialized carving. Accessory tools like clamps and files make finishing easier and assist in holding the wood while you carve. You do not need every tool in every size but a wide variety is a great idea, so build your workshop as you have funds available.

Woodcarving can be hard on the hands and cause fatigue. Gripping the tools incorrectly and using new tools may hurt your hands, so strengthen them by doing stretches or squeezing a stress ball. Knives and other bladed tools, even files with dull edges, can cause cuts and grazes on your hands. Consider using whittling gloves or finger guards to protect your hands. After all, cutting yourself will leave you out of action and unable to continue carving until your hand has healed fully. A pair of safety glasses do not go amiss either, especially when chip carving, as wood shavings and chips fly everywhere and may hit you in the eye, which can cause permanent damage.

Several types of wood are available for carving with the most popular options remaining softwood. Balsa, butternut, and basswood are suitable for beginners, although you may want to challenge yourself by using a harder wood like cherry or tupelo. Wood can be expensive, especially if it is hard to come by or a high-demand variety. Always practice your cuts on cheaper wood and only use more expensive wood once you master the new techniques. Be aware of grain patterns when purchasing wood so that your piece does not contain pith or too many interlocked patterns. There is nothing worse than ruining an expensive wood with an improper cutting from insufficient practice.

Sharp tools are crucial for proper carving as dull knives can split the wood or slip and cause unintended damage. A dull tool requires more force to move through the wood, which also ruins the finished product. Sharpening stones assist in keeping blades in good condition. Oil, diamond, water, ceramic, and Arkansas stones are available for sharpening and each has unique characteristics. Most carvers will have a range of sharpening stones to shape, sharpen, and polish the blade. Select a set of stones that work best for your tools and store the stones properly for longer usage.

A masterpiece is only as good as its finish. Finishing the piece requires careful sanding and application of a finishing medium. These mediums create a surface finish or penetrate the wood. Penetrating finishes are a better option as they nourish the wood and enter into the grain, while surface finishes produce a film over the wood. However, both types of finishes are suitable and you will know the best one for your piece. Be mindful of which finishes work with each other and those that cannot be used together. Try a variety of finishes on different pieces to identify the ones you like best.

Several projects are found in the first two chapters, as well as chapter 8. These projects contain various designs that span across all the new techniques. Some of the projects combine the techniques for more complex projects. Now that you have the knowledge and tools, grab a piece of wood, and start practicing your wood carving skills. Do not worry about failing, rather, try and try again, until you master every cut. You can only learn if you make mistakes, so take every opportunity to improve your carving expertise.

Throughout this book, I shared 15 secrets to wood carving. Remember these secrets and apply their teachings to carve successfully. If you enjoyed reading this book and have greater knowledge after learning these secrets, then please leave a review on Amazon.

References

Arbor Day Foundation. (n.d.). Anatomy of a
tree.
https://www.arborday.org/trees/treegui
de/anatomy.cfm

Arnold, E. (2014). How to varnish wood… so it
looks really good. The Daily Bark.
https://www.wood-finishes-
direct.com/blog/how-to-varnish-wood-
so-it-looks-really-good/

Art of Making. (n.d.). Tool: flat chisel. The Art
of Making in Antiquity.
http://www.artofmaking.ac.uk/explore/
tools/4/Flat-Chisel

Baylor, C. (2019a). How to apply a lacquer
finish. The Spruce Crafts.
https://www.thesprucecrafts.com/how-
to-apply-a-lacquer-finish-3536491

Baylor, C. (2019b). How to apply finishing wax
to a wood finish. The Spruce Crafts.
https://www.thesprucecrafts.com/apply
ing-a-paste-wax-wood-finish-3536492

Baylor. C. (2019c). How to use a skew chisel
    woodturning tool. The Spruce Crafts.
    https://www.thesprucecrafts.com/how-
    to-use-a-skew-chisel-3536930

Baylor, C. (2020a). Applying polyurethane for
    a durable, beautiful finish. The Spruce
    Crafts.
    https://www.thesprucecrafts.com/apply
    ing-polyurethane-for-durable-beautiful-
    finish-3536497

Baylor, C. (2020b). How to apply a beautiful
    shellac finish on woodwork. The Spruce
    Crafts.
    https://www.thesprucecrafts.com/get-
    beautiful-woodworking-finishes-with-
    shellac-3536494

Best Wood Carving Tools. (n.d.). Complete
    comprehensive guide for relief carving.
    https://www.bestwoodcarvingtools.com
    /the-complete-comprehensive-guide-
    for-relief-carving/

Duguay, C. (n.d.). Penetrating oil finishes.
    Canadian Woodworking.
    https://www.canadianwoodworking.co
    m/tipstechniques/penetrating-oil-
    finishes

Duncan, B. (2017). Great gouges: the essential tool kit. Woodcarving Illustrated. http://woodcarvingillustrated.com/blog/2017/09/04/great-gouges-essential-tool-kit/

Ellenwood, E. (2008). The Complete Book of Woodcarving. East Petersburg, PA: Fox Chapel Publishing.

Ellenwood, E. (2017). Anatomy of wood. Woodcarving Illustrated. http://woodcarvingillustrated.com/blog/2017/09/18/anatomy-of-wood/

George Hill Timber. (n.d.). Understanding wood grain. https://georgehill-timber.co.uk/blog/understanding-wood-grain/

Infinity Tools. (n.d.). Choosing the proper mallet. https://www.infinitytools.com/blog/2016/05/09/choosing-the-proper-mallet/

Irish, L. S. (n.d.a). Incised carving. lsirish. https://lsirish.com/tutorials/woodcarving-tutorials/woodcarving-fundamentals-techniques/specialized-techniques/incised-carving/

Irish, L. S. (n.d.b). Intaglio carving. lsirish.
    https://lsirish.com/tutorials/woodcarvi
    ng-tutorials/woodcarving-
    fundamentals-techniques/specialized-
    techniques/intaglio-carving/

Johnson, D. B. (2006a). Intaglio. Canadian
    Woodworking.
    https://www.canadianwoodworking.co
    m/plans-projects/intaglio

Johnson, D. B. (2006b). The bluenose.
    Canadian Woodworking.
    https://www.canadianwoodworking.co
    m/plans-projects/bluenose

Joslyn, C. (2017). Sea shell paperweight.
    Woodcarving Illustrated.
    http://woodcarvingillustrated.com/blog
    /2017/07/06/sea-shell-paperweight/

Leenhouts, M. (2018). Chip-carved wine bottle
    holder. Woodcarving Illustrated.
    http://woodcarvingillustrated.com/blog
    /2018/04/23/chip-carved-wine-bottle-
    holder/

Lie-Nielsen. (n.d.). Fishtail chisels.
    https://www.lie-
    nielsen.com/nodes/4173/fishtail-chisels

McKenzie, B. (2016). Stylish birdhouse. Woodcarving Illustrated. http://woodcarvingillustrated.com/blog/2016/03/01/stylish-birdhouse/

Minwax. (n.d.). Staining interior wood. https://www.minwax.com/how-to-finish-wood/staining-wood/#:~:text=Stain%20can%20be%20applied%20with,fill%20deep%20pores%20with%20stain.

Pye, C. (2017a). Line carving: three simple styles. Woodcarving Illustrated. http://woodcarvingillustrated.com/blog/2017/09/29/line-carving-three-simple-styles/

Pye, C. (2017b). Basic relief techniques. Woodcarving Illustrated. http://woodcarvingillustrated.com/blog/2017/11/27/basic-relief-techniques/

Schroeder, R. (2010). Files, rasps, and rifflers. Woodcarving Illustrated. http://woodcarvingillustrated.com/blog/2010/01/24/files-rasps-rifflers/

Schroeder, R. (2017a). All about chisels, gouges, and v-tools part 1. Woodcarving Illustrated.

http://woodcarvingillustrated.com/blog
/2017/04/18/all-about-chisels-gouges-
and-v-tools-part-1/

Schroeder, R. (2017b). All about clamps &
vises. Woodcarving Illustrated.
http://woodcarvingillustrated.com/blog
/2017/12/08/all-about-clamps-vises/

Sharpening Supplies. (n.d.). Arkansas Stone
FAQ's.
https://www.sharpeningsupplies.com/A
rkansas-Stone-FAQs-W169.aspx

Sharpening Supplies. (n.d.). Selecting a
sharpening stone.
https://www.sharpeningsupplies.com/D
ifference-in-Sharpening-Stone-
Materials-W51C116.aspx

Sharpening Supplies. (n.d.). What is the
difference between ceramic stones and
ceramic water stones?
https://www.sharpeningsupplies.com/
What-is-the-difference-between-
ceramic-stones-and-ceramic-water-
stones-W135.aspx

Stewart, W. (2020). Best oils for wood 2020 -
Reviews and buyer's guide. Wood
Improve.

https://woodimprove.com/best-oils-for-wood/

Woodcarver. (2018). Best hook knives for easy spoon carving. Best Wood Carving Tools. https://www.bestwoodcarvingtools.com/best-hook-knives-for-easy-spoon-carving/

Woodcraft. (2016). Wood for carvers. https://www.woodcraft.com/blog_entries/wood-for-carvers

Woodworking Toolkit. (2020). Chip carving: Ultimate guides for beginners - tools, tips, resources & more. https://woodworkingtoolkit.com/chip-carving/

Workshop Companion. (n.d.). Wood Grain. http://workshopcompanion.com/KnowHow/Design/Nature_of_Wood/1_Wood_Grain/1_Wood_Grain.htm

Images in order of appearance:

https://pixabay.com/photos/clog-isolated-special-craft-dutch-18399/

https://pixabay.com/photos/carving-wood-mantel-hands-96088/

https://pixabay.com/photos/tool-wood-work-edit-carve-craft-1364892/

https://burst.shopify.com/photos/wood-working-tools-laid-on-a-bench?q=wood+mallet

https://pixabay.com/photos/annual-rings-tree-tree-grates-wood-2924661/

https://pixabay.com/photos/brush-oil-wood-paint-creativeness-5095758/

https://pixabay.com/photos/wood-figure-mouse-holzfigur-9247/

https://pixabay.com/photos/friend-carving-wood-friendship-1753870/

https://pixabay.com/vectors/border-decoration-design-element-40894/

https://pixabay.com/photos/bird-wood-carving-color-988415/

9 781951 035969